S0-ARC-512

Essential
Neil Young

First published in Great Britain in 1998 by Chameleon Books

an imprint of André Deutsch Ltd

76 Dean Street

London W1V 5HA

André Deutsch Ltd is a VCI plc company

www.vci.co.uk

Design: Neal Townsend for JMP Ltd.

Picture research: Karen Tucker for JMP Ltd.

1 3 5 7 9 10 8 6 4 2

Printed and bound in Great Britain by Jarrold Book Printing, Norfolk

A catalogue record for this book is available from the British Library

ISBN 0 233 99412 2

Essential Neil Young

STEVE GRANT

For Meg and William

and for Clare Downs
(no more aluminium foil please!)

Acknowledgements

This book owes a debt of thanks to the following. First of all to my friend Peter Silverton, whose *Essential Elvis* was the template for this study and who acted with decent haste upon my initial suggestion. Unfortunately, none of the resulting deficiencies can be laid at his door.

A special tribute must go to Andrew Bell of *World In Action*; Brad Auerbach of Marina del Rey, California and Kuala Lumpur, Malaysia; Ross Fortune and Derek Adams at *Time Out* for their ideas, enthusiasm, and book and record libraries. I would also like to thank Jill Tulip, Andy Rossiter, Mike Ellison, Katie O'Dowd, Simon Chappell, Tim Arthur, Linton Chiswick, Laura Lee Davies, Oliver Reed (a musician friend of my son's, not the boozy actor), Kathy Norrish, Ernie Eban, Peter Paphides, Geoff Andrew, Tony Elliott, Mike Hardwick, Garry Mulholland, Wally Hammond, Tom Charity, Paul Charman, Mark Borkowski, Nichola Coulthard and, for nearly thirty years of loyal friendship and forbearance, Jane Edwardes.

I would also like to pay a debt of thanks to Nicholas Royle for his encouragement of my creative writing over the last few years, even though the only Neil Young he idolizes is the one who scored Manchester City's Cup Final winner in 1969.

Though they are thanked in the bibliography, this book wouldn't have been possible without the work of the true keepers of the Neil Young flame: Alan Jenkins at *Broken Arrow* magazine, the awesome scholarship of Pete Long, the early pioneering work of John Einarson, and last but not least the indefatigable efforts of Johnny Rogan, writer, publisher and all-round Neil Young obsessive.

Thanks also to Mal and John at JMP.

contents

DON'T CRY NO TEARS

First released: Zuma (Reprise) **November 1975**

Though it wasn't finally recorded until the mid-1970s, Don't Cry No Tears seems the only place to start this personal journey through the past and present of Neil Young. This was one of a batch of around 30 songs which Neil wrote in his adolescence, growing up in optimistic, post-war, baby-boom Canada. Neil was born two 'years' before me, but our difference in months is a mere 14. He was actually conceived before the end of the last War and born in Toronto in November, 1945. I had to wait until Hitler allowed my parents to resume their wartime marriage in earnest and emerged into the coldest winter in years, midway through January, 1947, in south east London.

History will not note the proximity of these two births but one of the themes of this book is that music has the power to cross all barriers, and that our cherished stars are at once so far away from us, so obviously removed from us by their fame and fortunes and lifestyles. And yet through their creations, through their own life-changes and rites of passage they have this enormous, life enhancing ability to draw us close to them and, finally, hopefully, to the people that we cherish, be they friends, lovers or our children. I have spent long enough interviewing, visiting with and writing about famous people to know that perhaps it's best if the gaps remain, otherwise that way stalking and fan-obsession lie: in the same way that continually and blindly revisiting one's past can be a tricky business. There's an amusing episode of *Hancock's Half Hour* which illustrates this: Tony Hancock decides to hold a twenty-years-on reunion party for his old army buddies, a trio of supposed womanizers, pranksters and hard drinkers. When they turn up one by one, they are in turn an ulcerated, hen-pecked, teetotal bank clerk reduced to drinking weak tea and lettuce sandwiches; an addled-brained dodderer with no memory at all; and a vicar, once called 'Ginger' for his splendid head of red-hair, who's gone completely bald. I don't know if the Young family ever saw the much-exported Hancock in Toronto or Onemee or Winnipeg, but I do know that Neil Young's entire career has been one of turning away from the past, of putting away old projects, of only recording and releasing tracks when the time is right, of generously embracing new forms and new artists: maybe Neil is conscious of how futile Elvis Presley's attitude of contempt, envy and disgruntlement to the Beatles was.

Elvis plays as big a part in Young's early musical consciousness as he does in those of anyone who grew up at the time when rock music was beginning to exert its hold over the young on both sides of the Atlantic. Young people today (sorry, it's the last time I'll use that phrase) sometimes get rightly irritated by the 1960s generation's obsession with their own pasts: it's partly understandable envy, partly a feeling that not enough of permanence came out of all that change and radicalism, maybe that it's even been reversed. But growing up in the late 1950s and early 1960s was a unique and dizzying experience: now my kids can tell me to turn down Jimi Hendrix or debate the relative merits of Teenage Fanclub, Blur and Oasis, and I'll know what they are talking about. Hey, I've even got the albums. Back then we had the generation gap, which came to my home in a hurry. My dad believed in 'Bing' and an Irish chanteuse called Ruby Murray who sang things like The Key To My Heart, the perkily

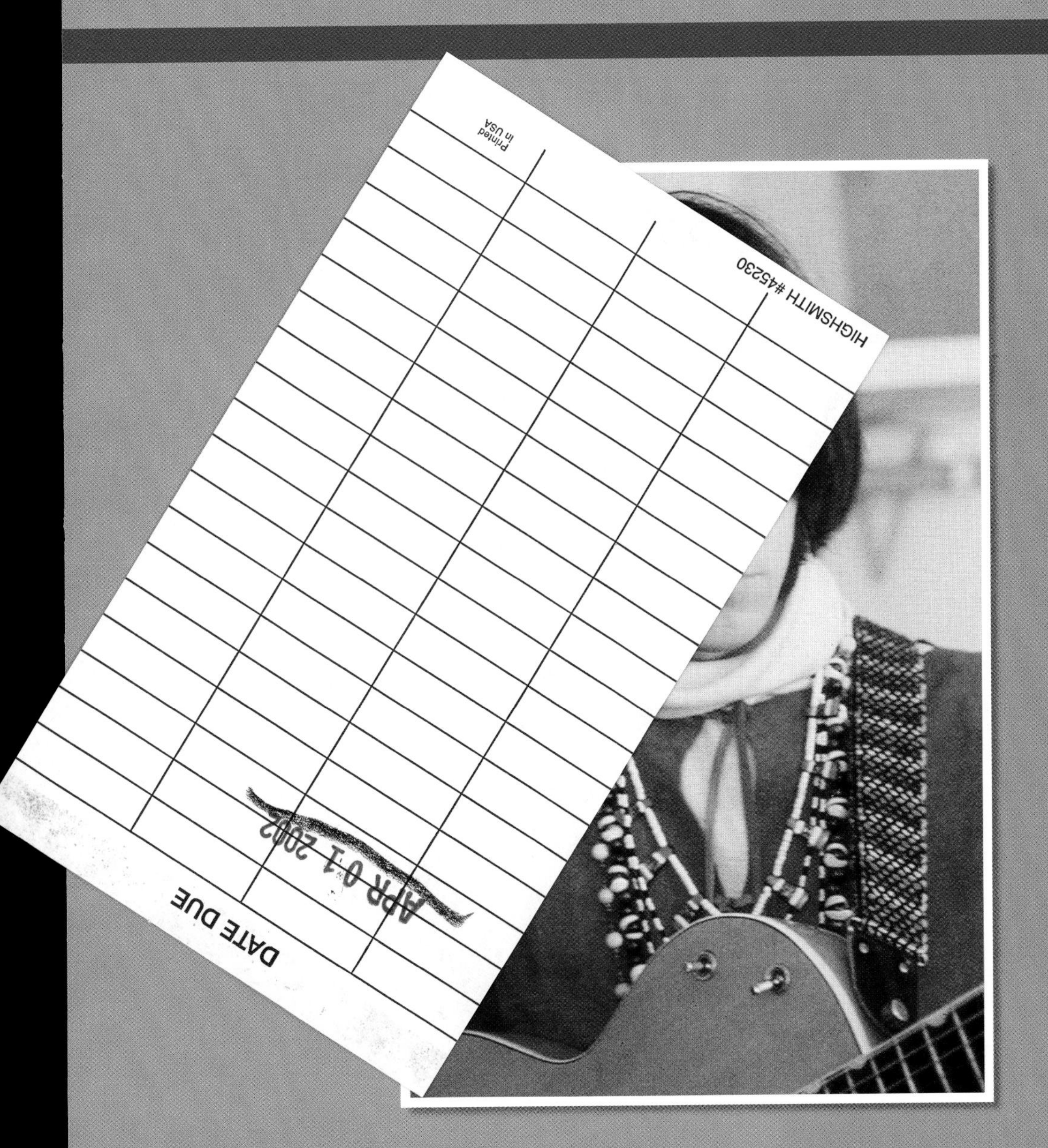

wholesome Alma Cogan, or someone who still gives me the shudders called Anne Shelton. He brought back a serious collection of Italian 78s from the war and refused to speak to my mother, who was always more cool, for a week when she bought a copy of Elvis's It's Now Or Never and then, God forbid, Surrender, his admittedly pretty ropy Anglicized version of my dad's favourite ballad of all, Sorrento. I can still remember the groans of horror at the Beatles' first television appearance, the disgust at what now looks almost like a set of short-back-and-sides haircuts, the time I actually left home because dad always watched the anodyne good-cop series *Dixon Of Dock Green* on Saturday evenings and wouldn't let me see the Rolling Stones make their debut on *Thank Your Lucky Stars*. Luckily, I returned from the recently-completed M1 turnoff before they actually noticed I'd gone missing.

Neil says that he got his first real charge from watching Elvis on the famous *Ed Sullivan*

Show special. Elvis affected us all: walking down our street one summer day, still young enough to think that sex was something the coalman brought the coal in, I heard All Shook Up coming out of someone's window: that sultry, horny voice, those groans of anguish, that subdued honky-tonk rhythm. All Shook Up. You bet. Like Little Richard, Ricky Nelson, Fabian, the Everly Brothers, Neil's early twanging guitar hero Duane Eddy or even our own home-grown Cliff Richard And The Shadows, this was our music. It didn't belong to our parents.

Young's early days seem both far more tranquil and more disrupted than my own: he moved house a lot; his father and mother split up when he was barely in his teens; he survived the polio epidemic which hit in 1951, but only just; he never did well at school after he decided, around the age of 14, that he wanted to make music his life. He was even bullied, although older brother Bob usually chipped in to save the day. He did, however, once famously clout a class thug over the head with a large textbook. He was also popular with girls, who liked his long legs and jet black hair, his sensitivity and 'intensity', the most common adjective used to describe him by contemporaries in John Einarson's superb piece of original rock research, *Don't Be Denied: Neil Young – The Canadian Years*. But despite the real social disadvantages in this period, he doesn't seem to have been too adversely affected by his parents' divorce, indeed it gave him an additional cachet with school friends already impressed by his quirky sense of humour and love of nature. One of Neil's youthful favourite singles was Farmer John, written and performed by Don and Dewey in 1959 and a Premieres' Top 20 hit some years later. He eventually recorded a version on Ragged Glory in 1990, but Neil was very much a nature boy from the time he earnt his first money keeping chickens and selling the eggs. He clearly enjoyed his youthful, seemingly idyllic fishing trips and toboggan rides, games of street hockey and battles across frozen lakes. Neil's father, Scott, a distinguished fiction writer whose autobiographical *Neil And Me* remains a fascinating if necessarily partial account of their relationship, became a distinguished sports scribe and broadcaster. In 1988, he was inducted into the Hockey Hall Of Fame, seven years before Neil made it to the rock 'n' roll equivalent. Despite Neil's early accomplishments on the golf course (he once famously used to trade golf lessons for guitar lessons) and the hockey stick that hangs in his Broken Arrow ranch today, Young was one of those skinny kids who was always playing the guitar and never wanted to make it to quarterback or to the national hockey squad.

By 1958, Neil had acquired his first stringed instrument, an Arthur Godfrey plastic ukulele, an axe-ette which produced a sound so naff that Woody Allen made stand-up jokes about taking potential girlfriends back to hear his Arthur Godfrey Hawaiian guitar music. With the help of his independent, tough-talking mother, Rassy, Neil moved from the uke to a similar model banjo and finally to a Harmony Monterey acoustic guitar that his brother Bob thought was rather 'uncertain in tone'. Scott recalls the days spent mulling over sheets of cowboy music, so familiar from my own youth around this time from 1959 and beyond: it's an abiding tragedy of so many of us that we tried and failed to learn the guitar around the same time as Eric Clapton, Pete Townshend, Keith Richard and John Lennon. How many of us gave up when faced with those guitar manuals, those early models that came cheap and had stops that you could press down on the strings to make a chord, those 'real guitars' that brought bleeding fingers and blistered thumbs?

Neil went through a few high school bands: the Jades, who only played one gig and who featured instrumentals from the time like the Ventures' Walk, Don't Run, Perfidia, and (good job, my dad didn't know!) Sorrento; then the more established Esquires, from the Fort Rouge district of Winnipeg; and finally with his close friend Ken Koblun and drummer and classmate Jack Harper, The Squires – who performed regularly from February 1963 until April 1965, in a variety of local clubs such as Cellar, Twilight Zone and the Town and Country Club.

Though Britons and Americans have always looked down on Canada – Peter Ustinov once described Toronto as 'New York built by the Swiss' – it had the advantage of being open to sounds from both America and naturally, given its status as a former colony, Britain. It also had a healthy folk and country scene, not least because of the large numbers of Scots and Irish who made such a massive contribution to the country's fabric. This must be why one of Neil's earliest and most enduring influences was Hank Marvin, lead guitarist of Cliff Richard's backing group, The Shadows, and massively successful instrumentalists in their own right with a string of UK hits from the ageless, haunting Apache, to FBI, Man Of Mystery (the theme from the Edgar Wallace film mysteries), Wonderful Land and Dance On, some of which featured in Young's early repertoire as a budding rhythm guitar player. Marvin was famous for perfecting his 'tremolo arm' technique on the Fender Stratocaster, which he used to give the notes a ringing, arpeggiated sound, moving the lever as he played and dancing in step at the same time. Bruce Welch, Marvin's co-guitarist in the band, gave the group's output a clearly defined strumming pattern.

Along with The Shadows, early songs covered also included the Tornados' world hit, Telstar, Wipe Out by the Surfaris, with that drum break that every kid in my class tried to play on the desks, Jan And Dean's Surfin' USA, and Runaway by Del Shannon – whose falsetto yodels could be heard by most of our neighbours on Sunday nights when my dad used an early Elizabethan model tape recorder to record Radio Luxembourg's Top 20 with Brian Matthew. I tried to pass the end results off as a collection of records but my mates weren't really fooled by the overlapping of the tunes nor by the appalling sound which rose and fell away continuously. Despite their massive popularity in the UK, Cliff and The Shadows did minimal damage to the US charts which, prior to the advent of the Beatles, only seemed to respond to British novelty records, mainly jazz hits like Acker Bilk's Stranger On The Shore and Kenny Ball and His Jazzmen's dangerously un-American Midnight In Moscow.

There was also the usual collection of folkies, an early sign of Neil's ability to fuse different musical styles into one unique voice: Clementine, Oh Susannah, She'll Be Coming 'Round The Mountain, Frankie And Johnny and even the early Bob Dylan song, Don't Think Twice, It's Alright.

DON'T CRY NO TEARS

It was The Shadows who most influenced The Squires' only, locally recorded (on the Vee label) and played single The Sultan, (b/w Aurora), but by 1964 the band had become sufficiently inspired by the influx of Beatlemania to incorporate the Fab Four's material into their newly vocalized act. Neil's debut as a singer in public was his answer to John Lennon's screeched-out Money (written, incidentally, by Bradford and Gordy) and It Won't Be Long Now, both belted out in the cafeteria of the Kelvin High School. Then as sometimes now, Neil's voice wasn't a hit; in fact, one early recording engineer advised him: 'You're a good guitarist, son, but you'll never make it as a singer.' The Squires even donned Beatles wigs to wow the local girls and evade the strictures against 'long-hairs'.

One of Young's earliest influences was Randy Bachman, a local guitarist and the first to assimilate Marvin's style of playing, a man whose band The Guess Who would have a North American hit in 1965 with Johnny Kidd And The Pirates' UK rocker, Shakin' All Over. By then, Neil had graduated from a Gibson Les Paul that used to give him electric shocks to his famous orange Gretsch, which appeared on an early poster from the Flamingo Club-Tavern, Fort William: 'Back by popular demand: Neil Young And The Squires', after the outfit had started to play in this Ontario railway terminus and grain station town late in 1964. The band are pictured in the matching outfits of the day – black vests, open-necked white-shirts and matching dark V-necked sweaters – at a time when even the Beatles were pulled into corduroy-suited, neckless-jacketed line.

Another enthusiastically received import at the time were The Kinks, who had initial success in the States before a strange altercation with a photographer and some cross-Pond linguistic confusion over the word 'fag'. Their leader Ray Davies once told me about the horrors of mid-1960s dress codes: 'When we made our debut on *Ready Steady Go* in 1964, they made us wear these itchy Thames Green velvet suits. I was grinning madly at the camera but I was in so much agony with my back that I was almost collapsing. They actually plugged up the gap in my teeth because you weren't allowed such facial blemishes on TV in those days. They put a cap in so I looked like Bugs Bunny. We always had image problems: after that they stuck us in red hunting jackets.'

And so to Don't Cry No Tears, which has been through several changes and rechristenings in the period between its inception when Young was but 14 years old and its appearance on record: to I Wonder (not to be confused with the Robert Cray ballad of the same name), and to Don't Pity Me Babe. It's a simple, jockstrap-heavy song of male pride very similar in tone and structure to early Beatles songs, notably Not A Second Time, and You Can't Do That on A Hard Day's Night, but certainly as it appears on Zuma it has a ringing tone which conjures up both The Shadows and The Byrds. The lyric of I Wonder (1964) adds the sentiment '*Well, I never cared too much anyway/Well, I guess that I'll forget her someday.*' But the final version is more adamant: *'Don't cry no tears around me'*. Basically, you're cheating on me, but you don't know what you're missing. NY

SUGAR MOUNTAIN

First released: Decade (Reprise) **November 1977**

Featured on various B-sides, this wistful classic was written in the Victoria Hotel very early in the morning of Young's nineteenth birthday, spent in residence at the Flamingo Club in Fort William, Ontario, off the aptly named Thunder Bay. This is a song about innocence and its loss, about growing up and leaving home, about independence and personal turbulence. Young was born on 12 November, a birthday which he shares with musicians including Grace Kelly, jazz trumpeter Buck Clayton, Russian composer Alexander Borodin and Neil's sometime collaborator, Booker T Jones. Not to mention one Charles Manson *(see Revolution Blues entry).*

Though it's often been dismissed as trite and, hey, even 'sugary' (get away!), Sugar Mountain is a beautifully delicate and sombre piece, a companion to I Am A Child from the last Buffalo Springfield album, Last Time Around, where Young's voice takes on the quiet, almost humiliated tones of an infant sent to his room for bad behaviour. Young was in the middle of a road trip with his band The Squires, in his mother's bad books for what father Scott Young recalls in a letter from his estranged wife, Rassy: 'Neil has decided to follow your advice and become a dropout.'

In 1964, Neil would already have been well acquainted with the Burl Ives children's classic, Big Rock Candy Mountain, in which *'lemonade springs and the bluebird sings in the soda water fountain'*. For Young, childhood is a carnival of barkers and coloured balloons, of candy floss, friends and parental security, giving way always to the thought of 'leaving there too soon', a thought finally reinforced by the guilt of first-time cigarettes and the 'glares' of adolescent competition.

Critics should pause before they confuse triteness with simplicity, however. The poet Thom Gunn, writing about The Beatles' Eleanor Rigby, picked on the lines describing her funeral, 'buried alone with her name'. 'Nobody came', said Gunn, 'was both a fact and a comment on that fact'. So too, Young's song is one of his best visual narratives, spare and awkward, in keeping with the times that were a-changing in his life.

Loss of innocence is, of course, an enduring artistic theme: it oozes from the Graham Greene short story about a man who returns to find a love note in a tree, written during his childhood. It turns out to be an obscene drawing. Less graphically, poets like William Blake, Thomas Hardy and AE Housman used the same simple ballad style to conjure up the void that we all have to cross, whether it be leaving behind 'blue remembered hills' or no longer 'piping down the valleys wild'. More chilling, of course, is the link between the murder of John Lennon and JD Salinger's classic novel of reluctant ageing, *The Catcher In The Rye*. Lennon's killer, Mark Chapman, so identified with Holden Caulfield's blast of childhood rage against the 'phonies' of the adult world that he wanted it to be a Bible for the young and picked it up for the umpteenth time minutes after blowing Lennon away.

Young's had his own brushes with obsessive fans, as he told Nick Kent in 1994: 'Oh yeah, I've had some real nutcases looking for answers that I couldn't begin to give 'em. There's only one way to deal with them: ignore them and escape them as quickly as possible.' NY

NOWADAYS CLANCY CAN'T EVEN SING

First released: Buffalo Springfield (Atco) **January 1967**

Clancy is a pivotal song, both in Neil's writing career and in his own personal history. Without it, Buffalo Springfield may not have happened, but then his whole progress between the time of The Squires and his arrival on the LA scene big-time was marked with accident and fortuitous coincidence.

By June 1965, Neil and a musical buddy had arrived at Scott Young's apartment in Toronto, bent on a change of scene and musical atmosphere. Toronto was the centre of a thriving and diverse club scene at the time, boasting clubs that embraced folk, jazz, rock and country, clubs that housed everyone from the tentative, learning Joni Mitchell to the outrageous R&B heavy Ronnie Hawkins, whose group The Hawks later transformed popular musical history as The Band. According to John Einarson and contrary to what Hawkins has said, Neil didn't actually see Hawkins play, but the two must have crossed each other's path. Hawkins is one of rock's enduring wagsters, not only because he told The Band/Hawks that, despite the bad wages and hours, they'd 'see more pussy than a toilet seat', but because he once claimed to have 'been to orgies Nero would have walked out of'.

The Squires were coming to a bitter end, and a solo gig in Winnipeg hardly restored confidence in his early 'white wailer' voice. Neil's desire to move to Toronto was not just about going up in the pecking order of fame but specifically to make fresh contact with a guy who'd seen his outfit play at the Fort Dimension in Fort William and was impressed. The musician, blonde, long haired, good looking, possessed of an excellent voice and with a track record in folk harmony, was called Stephen Stills. Around this time, Neil had become increasingly influenced by Bob Dylan's electrification that year with Highway 61 Revisited, while bands such as The Byrds, The Beach Boys, and The Rolling Stones were also much more in his sight-lines (as was avant-garde jazz musician Sun Ra, who Neil was turned on to in Yorketown, the Toronto equivalent of Greenwich Village). This is a strange period for him; a bit, dare I say it, like the rock equivalent of Hitler's Vienna period; full of cheap burgers, crash pads, drugs, an early epilepsy scare, desultory one-off gigs, a botched recording audition with Elektra and a very brief reincarnation (with Ken Koblun) as Four To Go. But throughout the bleakness, there remains the visit to Greenwich Village in New York, Neil searching for Stills at 171 Thompson Street, meeting his roommate Richie Furay instead and Neil teaching him Clancy on the spot. Neil's good at that: a journalist friend recalls a slight depression in a carpet in Daniel Lanois's home-cum-studio in the French Quarter of New Orleans—complete with a copy of John Kennedy Toole's novel, *Confederacy Of Dunces*, on the bedside table. Emmylou Harris, who Lanois was producing at the time, pointed at the depression and murmured: 'That's where Neil stood on tiptoe and played Wrecking Ball to me.'

Furay, Stills and Young, along with Dewey Martin and Bruce Palmer, were later to form Buffalo Springfield, after another very fortuitous meeting at some traffic lights on Hollywood's Sunset Boulevard. Clancy was the first notable connection, one no doubt reinforced when Young met the 19-year-old Bruce Palmer in January, 1966. Palmer was a respected bassist with a leading Toronto band, Jack London And The Sparrow. He was, more importantly, ready to use

a hungry fellow countryman in his current outfit, The Mynah Birds, led by Ricky James Matthews, a black Mick Jagger impressionist who later found fortune and fame as Rick James. This detour led Young and his new-found group, in which he had to take a back seat for a change, to Detroit and a bizarre recording session for Tamla Motown in which Smokey Robinson is known to have participated – in the wings, at least. In April, 1995, Young told *Musician Forum* magazine: 'We were the first white group that Motown had. Rick James was our lead singer and the rest of us were white. It was a pretty cool band. We used to do a lot of Rolling Stones-type stuff, and then Rick and I wrote a couple of things together. I remember I had this acoustic 12-string on, playing these country kind of licks, and it was cool – this *was* '65. The drums were nailed down. We used their drummer.' The sessions, which ended up dominated vocally by three session singers, had recently been relocated, but fortunately for Neil, as it turned out, Tamla lost their interest in The Mynah Birds when James was arrested for desertion from the US Navy.

Young played Clancy on his unsuccessful Elektra audition tape and had written it after the break up of The Squires and his subsequent frustrations on the solo and folk-rock circuit in Toronto. When Palmer and Young eventually decamped to Los Angeles, still looking for Stills, they were unaware that Stephen was not only in LA with Furay but that Furay had by now taught Stills Clancy as well and the two had discussed what an interesting guy Neil was. The meeting has become the stuff of legend, and apocryphally dated to April Fool's Day, 1966: on their way out of LA, heading towards San Francisco, Young and Palmer in the famous hearse (celebrated in Long May You Run) bumped into Stills and Furay at a red light, recognized each other (Stills was the first), embraced and no doubt screamed, 'Let's form a band.'

After bringing in Martin from the excellent Dillards on drums, and knocking them dead, particularly at Hollywood's celebrated night-spot the Whisky-A-Go-Go, Buffalo Springfield, who took their name from words on the side of a passing truck, were eventually snapped up by the predominantly black music label, Atlantic. Their first single was to have been a Stills song, but pressure from local radio stations made Atlantic reverse the order and lead with Clancy. The tensions between Stills and Young, which had been partially exorcized by savage guitar duels, resurfaced over the vocals. The downside of the progress of Clancy through the hearts and minds of Stills and Furay was that, by the time the group hit the recording studio, the two had worked out the vocals between them; 'which,' Neil told John Einarson, 'set the pattern'. Though Stills' For What It's Worth, a late addition to the album's listing, was undoubtedly the song of their debut album, Neil, who is credited with five compositions as opposed to Stills' seven, produced, overall, the more arresting, quirky material, notably the plaintive Out Of My Mind, with its slow, doom-laden guitar intro (reminiscent of Wrecking Ball from the later Freedom) and the jokey Flying On The Ground Is Wrong.

Clancy is the first recorded Neil Young groundbreaker, but Neil doesn't sing on it: the lead vocal is taken by Furay with Stills providing backing (at this time in LA, four-track recording was well established, eight-track possible, and all these songs were recorded with the backing track first and the vocals overdubbed, a new experience for Young). Those who have heard both usually prefer the haunting Young version, but Furay and Stills' musicality highlights one of the song's most arresting features, its ability in patches to sound like a straight composition for a Tony Bennett or even a Sinatra, the possibility even of strings. The song has a jerky, off-on melodic pattern and, despite lacking a recognisable hook, it sounds light years ahead of the mainly middle-period Beatles-influenced compositions on the rest of Buffalo Springfield. It also reflects the increasing influence of Dylan with its strange, indirect imagery: *'Who's putting sponge in the bells I once rung/And taken my gypsy before she's begun?'*

Clancy was a kid at Neil's high school, a typically untypical kid, awkward, unsocialized, gifted, different, a kid who one classmate quoted by John Einarson says was called 'Clancy Smith' and was afflicted by multiple sclerosis. But Clancy the song is about more generalized themes of frustration and rage at not being allowed to follow your dream, of not being accepted because you are different. I suppose there are lots of personal connecting points for me from this period: it was my first term at college, the first period spent since puberty, alone, away from home and in the company of girls who I thought, as Malcolm Muggeridge once said, 'could be folded into three'. And of the ironies and coincidences in Young's career here, I could counter that, without a chance meeting my father had in the street, I probably wouldn't even have attended a grammar school or university. The details are complicated and boring, but because a neighbour's son was going from a London comprehensive school to the local grammar, I, who had taken the wretched 11-plus and narrowly failed it, should also go to the grammar. After all, reasoned dad, I'd been doing very well at my Elephant and Castle secondary modern. Or so he managed to convince both the education authority and the school. It was a rough age to change schools, 14 – something Neil knew a lot about with his itinerant early home life – the bullying at my new school was truly horrifying. The sons of local accountants, solicitors and policemen engaging in charming acts which included making every boy in my class spit upon the same, baffled transgressor (I slunk away, big deal, but I'm still relieved and faintly proud). Setting fire to someone's shoes and pouring purple ink over them was another beauty. Once, I was the chosen subject for a thrashing and so terrified that I uncharacteristically bunked off school for a whole 48 hours. What particularly galls me to this day is that the kids who were threatening the beating had completely forgotten. Thank God for the education, which was formal, sadistic and first rate, even if my English master did denounce a visit to The Rolling Stones at the local Dunstable California ballroom in 1963 as dealing with 'the antichrists'.

Coincidence isn't always what it seems: Michael Caine still swears blind, truly I'm sure, that he got his career-launching part in Zulu when he was half out the door and his agent suddenly asked: 'Can you do posh?' But a friend of mine who teaches drama and once played drums on chairs for Marty Wilde tells me of the early pop mythologizing process. 'Marty worked as a night watchman in a lumber yard and at the time it was put about that Larry Parnes the great producer was riding home one night and heard this wonderful, beautiful song coming towards him from this corrugated iron fence. When he approached the wooden hut, there inside was Marty. Of course, it was complete bollocks. As Larry said years later, "He auditioned like everyone else." When we auditioned, he told our manager: "I'll take the singer but I'm not touching the rest." '

Ironically, the ultimate failure of Clancy on the radio networks accelerated the tensions already there in this band of all talents. Programmers didn't like the song's length, around half a minute more than the average single, or its lyrics which included the then still frowned-upon word 'damn', despite it being almost thirty years after Clark Gable first uttered it on celluloid in *Gone With The Wind*. What must have been more than galling for Young's tumescent ego was that while Clancy failed to even make an impact on the local charts, it was Stills' rejected tune, For What It's Worth, that gave the Springfield their first national top 10 hit, when it reached number seven in March, 1967. NY

MR. SOUL

First released: Buffalo Springfield Again (Atco) **December 1967**

Young may have been restricted to one rather desultory rocker, Burned, on the first album, but Mr. Soul makes for a punchy opening to the second album, even if Young's vocals are obliterated by the flashy guitars and the rock riff which is a shameless 'homage' to the Rolling Stones' '(I Can't Get No) Satisfaction'.

As David Downing points out in his intelligent biography, *A Dreamer Of Pictures: Neil Young, The Man And His Music,* this was one time when the instrumentals let down the voice and certainly the lyrics, which are an early example of Young at his darkly witty best, full of paranoid thoughts channelled into lines full of internal rhymes and monosyllabic directness: *'I was raised by the praise of a fan who said I upset her.'* Young seems to have realized that this song hadn't been accorded its full potential, reviving it not only on his live, acoustic Unplugged, where it is far simpler and more sinister, with a lone harmonica making far more point than all the fuzzy guitar fade-outs of the original. He's also performed a more relaxed concert version, which can be heard on *Year Of The Horse*, again using an acoustic guitar brought so memorably to the rock scene by Young with the Springfield, but sadly absent here.

It's been said that prostitution is non-existent in Los Angeles because if you can't score there then no hooker will take your money, anyway. It's an exaggeration, of course, now as it was back in the 1960s, but it does give an insight into the laughably-named City Of Angels which, as writers from Kenneth Anger to James Ellroy have demonstrated, is more accurately a city of perverts, wannabes and party animals. Buffalo Springfield, hardly less than Jim Morrison, were quick to find hordes of willing groupies attracted by their youthful good looks and by their quickly spiralling reputation as one of the best live acts in the state. Even Young was to say later, 'We were good, even great', even if he remains frustrated by the recording sessions, which used too much overdubbing of voices and often flattened out the sound. It was a common gripe, certainly from bands like The Beatles and the Stones, whose early television appearances were often wrecked by thin, tinny sound which gave no idea of how loud and tight the band were on stage.

This was a period of excess: a time before women's liberation and after sexual freedom when individuals like Young could literally take their pick at clubs such as the Whisky-A-Go-Go, where anything from downers, uppers, acid and dope to full-throttle blow-jobs were freely available. While Stills seemed to take it in his stride, for Young – already unsettled by the onset of his first serious epileptic fit, still too much of a romantic and a thinker to be much impressed by the offer of sex and drugs on a plate, someone who may have become rather puritanical having experienced his own father's home-wrecking adultery – sudden adulation was a mixed blessing. No wonder the cutting irony of this song's valediction, 'respectfully dedicated to the ladies of the Whisky-A-Go-Go and the women of Hollywood'.

What this song also demonstrates is the essentially dramatic nature of Young's lyric writing, the almost classical invocation *'Well hello, Mr. Soul,'* with its double-edged reference to Neil's inner peace of mind, his 'soul', and the 'soul' of the popular music of which he was by now an established part. By this time, he'd not only recorded in Detroit with Motown but even jammed in New York with Otis Redding, the all-time Soul Man (no disrespect to Sam and Dave, of course). As well as the general degeneracy of the scene, and Young's own health problems, he was beaten up by a cop after an unpleasant exchange and in late April 1968, while the Springfield were still basking in this album's success, he was busted in Topanga Canyon along with Eric Clapton, then touring with Cream, Richie Furay and new band member Jim Messina. The latter's presence in the band was itself a drug-related event, the bass player having been brought in after Bruce Palmer was deported back to Canada, a veteran of three separate convictions for marijuana possession.

By this time, Young had made clear his intention to pursue a solo career. Neil was later to return to the subject of drugs possession on an unreleased track for the 1985 Old Ways album, Time Off For Good Behaviour. The song discusses the fate of a 'brother' who was arrested for *'something I've smoked all my life'.* Indeed, Neil's older brother Bob was arrested for involvement in a hashish ring in early 1982, the amount in question was valued at around $5 million. Bob was given a seven year sentence, although the conviction was eventually quashed. Jim Jarmusch's *Year Of The Horse* includes footage from the 1976 World Tour, in which Neil is clearly shown sharing a joint or two with members of Crazy Horse, and when asked would he rather be a drunk or an addict replies, 'Both.' Good stuff and right on Neil, but it all seems a long way from Sugar Mountain. NY

BROKEN ARROW

First released: Buffalo Springfield Again (Atco) **December 1967**

Though Young seems to have kissed this elaborate closer to the Springfields' second and most adventurous album goodbye, it endures in his personal mythology: both as the name of the spacious Californian ranch where he now lives with wife Pegi, family and a considerable variety of livestock, and as the name of the world's best music fanzine, *Broken Arrow*, a quarterly publication of enormous literacy, enthusiasm and variety, edited by the formidable Alan Jenkins from his home in Bridgend, South Wales.

Broken Arrow, at six minutes 13 seconds, is by far the longest track on Buffalo Springfield Again, and by far the most musically ambitious, taking on the kind of orchestral experimentation and daring arrangements of The Beatles, culminating when they began laying down tracks for Sergeant Pepper's Lonely Heart's Club Band over a year before this album was finally released. Despite the posthumously released Last Time Around, this second album was effectively the band's swan song, as it was torn apart by stark contrasts of personality and musical taste, and by more worldly arguments about whose songs survived at a time when the Springfield had become increasingly aware of the lucrative market in composers' rights.

The love-hate relationship between Steven Stills and Young had been cemented on the stage at live gigs where their celebrated guitar soloing was edgy, vicious even, although Young later reminisced about the harmony created by his slow playing as opposed to Stills' more frenzied, uptempo soloings. The rivalry was cemented visually and in a manner relevant to this song: Stills on the right as the blonde haired cowboy, the guy who might have ridden point with Custer, as opposed to Young, tall, dark and thoughtful, and usually dressed in fringed jerkins or a Comanche war shirt. Neil's long-time affinity with native Americans was later to be refocused with Pocahontas and Cortez The Killer.

The 'broken arrow' of the main chorus is the Indian symbol of peace, an indication of what has been lost in war and in conflict. Young can afford to talk more objectively about this period in his life now, but Broken Arrow is an elegy imbued with a sense of deep bitterness at the loss of idealism, all the compromises and frustrations of the only period in his life when he was essentially a support player, despite the obvious superiority of his songwriting to every one else in Buffalo Springfield. His time with the band had been a mere eighteen months – it must have seemed much longer.

Broken Arrow took Young around one hundred takes to complete and Johnny Rogan notes that at least two parts of the song are listed in the Atlantic archives under the titles Ball Park and Theme Jazz. It also changes its signature back and forth between 4/4 and 3/4 time; unusual for Young's direct style of composition. It begins startlingly with a burst of screams, a live, rock version of Mr Soul sung by Stills with Furay's bursts of Chuck Berry duck-walking no doubt explaining the fans' increasing ecstasy. The first verse is concerned with the drawbacks of rock fame, opening with the starkly simple: *'The lights turned on/And the curtain fell down'* and taking in the cynical figure of the agent with his hired limousine waiting in the rain. No doubt a nod in the direction of Barry Friedman, the man who had got the Springfield together, only to be bought out by Brian Stone and Charlie Greene, music hustlers well know to Atco, the company division of Atlantic that finally signed the band for $22,000.

Friedman is honoured with a dedication on this album, while Broken Arrow is dedicated personally by Young to Ken Koblun, perhaps his closest Canadian friend, and many of the people he'd had to leave behind in his early quest for fame. The 'screams' section recalls The Byrds' equally questioning stance on the subject of musical celebrity in So You Want To Be A Rock 'N' Roll Star? while some of the use of distortion and echo on the piano and organ obviously reiterates the awesome close to Sergeant Pepper's A Day In The Life.

After the screams of Mr Soul comes a snatch of fractured concert noise, a bit too like A Day In The Life for its own good, and then fairground music, a distorted organ and a piano roll to bring in the second verse, which is concerned with the repressive nature of parenting: *'He'd seen that his brother had sworn on the wall'* and *'Don't mention babies at all'* being two of the more bracing sentiments, surely not a reference to mother Rassy's earlier expressed horror at Neil's decision to 'become a dropout'.

After more piano and an eerily lengthy silence comes the final verse, about a king and queen who marry to protect the peace of the realm but who may, we are meant to think, repent at leisure; after all, the queen has *'protected her king from the sun rays of dawn'.* Another verse is about compromise, be it in a band, growing up and feeling guilty or doing something for the good of others. Of course, Young wasn't exactly guiltless in the conflict inside and speedy disintegration of Buffalo Springfield: Stills said that Neil 'wasn't a team player', while after several slope-offs, including one at the time of the band's induction on to the wretched *Ed Sullivan Show*, Young was to part ways with Crosby, Stills and Nash in 1970. It might be the first time he'd part with the trio, but it wasn't to be the last; Neil famously parted company with Stills on tour as late as 1976, with the exhortation to, 'Eat a peach.' Glib or what?

The last verse concludes with some impressively funky jazz piano by Don Randi and an uncredited bass clarinet passage, and climaxes with an array of musical and social images probably hinting at the potential for creativity to overcome the restrictions of real life: concert halls, fairgrounds and ball parks, jazz improvisation and maybe even the rock arena, if only those damn girls would stop screaming. NY

CINNAMON GIRL

First released: Everybody Knows This Is Nowhere (Reprise) **May 1969**

Like so many first-time creators, Neil Young says he made his first solo album just so he could prove he was capable. Clearly he was more than merely capable. It's one of his personal favourites, which may just be a nostalgia for early days, but also recognizes the true quality of many of the tracks.

The album was co-produced by Jack Nitzche, the awesomely talented maverick arranger from Michigan who'd worked with everyone from Phil Spector to The Byrds, had co-written Needles And Pins with Sonny Bono (a huge hit for The Searchers in 1964), is responsible for the music behind cult-movie *Performance* (1970) and, four years later, *The Exorcist*. Nitzche produced the ambitious Broken Arrow during Young's Buffalo Springfield days, but this was the first time Nitzche had Young to himself, so to speak. Ryland Cooder, as he was then known, the supremely gifted guitar player whose eclecticism rivals that of Young, is also on the record, accompanied by two loan-outs from Poco, bassist Jim Messina and drummer George Grantham. Nitzche was also a literal key player in the early Crazy Horse line-up, writing and playing piano on the excellent Long Dead Train, featured on the Performance soundtrack and later on Crazy Horse's first album in 1971, which also included a version of Dance, Dance, Dance, a Young song he's never put on record himself.

Another key player in Neil Young's early career was Elliot Roberts, Joni Mitchell's manager when Young approached him to handle his solo career. Roberts, a Bronx-born graduate of the William Morris mailroom in New York, admired Young's sense of humour, liked him and remains his manager to this day, a man who obviously knows how to handle his charge (with a good deal of wit and a very long lead). A third major player was David Briggs, a drifter from Wyoming who fell into record production in the mid-1960s on Bill Cosby's label, Tetragrammaton, and got to know Young when he offered him a lift. Briggs has a co-production credit on the album which marked the beginning of a long association with Young and with Crazy Horse.

For his second solo outing, Young teamed up with Crazy Horse, having met them after guesting alongside Danny Whitten, Ralph Molina and Billy Talbot at the Whisky-A-Go-Go in 1968. They were then part of The Rockets, they are now, of course, Neil's stomach and lungs. He has referred to them in the past as masters of Zen, not only allowing himself to find his own emotional centre within the music but allowing him to get to the kind of trance-like state in which he claims only real enjoyment and musical freedom comes. After Danny Whitten's death and Nils Lofgren's later solo departure, Young was lucky enough to find an adequate replacement in Frank 'Poncho' Sampedro for the interlocking, interchangeable relationship of rhythm and lead guitars.

This rapturous, timeless song not only predates the Spice Girls by at least a quarter of a century and is the first that Neil Young played with Crazy Horse. It's also the first record by Young that I heard, as a post-graduate student in the Manchester of the very early 1970s. Buffalo Springfield, Young's first major outfit, had passed me by; in fact, I remember a music scene that was somewhat xenophobic in its tastes, apart from Dylan and The Band, who had

crept through to the north west of England both together and separately: The Beatles (natch), The Rolling Stones (ditto), Jimi Hendrix, Led Zeppelin. I was living in the usual student house, and one day early in 1971 a blonde-haired Geordie whose name now escapes me brought round a bunch of left-field West Coast recordings: there was the Doors' Strange Days, the less creepy but equally organ-driven Electric Music For The Mind And Body by Country Joe And The Fish, Love's Da Capo, the Grateful Dead's American Beauty and Everybody Knows This Is Nowhere. Less portentous than The Doors, less majestic than the Dead, less wantonly cool than The Fish, less swaggering than Arthur Lee's Love, Neil's album came complete with engaging cover image. I love that initial shot of the man, hair coal-black, backed by mountains and cloud, lean, rangy, left arm up against the old oak tree like he was trying to push it over. The location is believed to be Berryhill, West Tulsa, where a horseshoe now decorates the tree. His plaid shirt and black tee-shirt look more clean than the stuff he now drowns in during live gigs. Less of a grunge biker look than a fresh-faced, at-home-after-the-semester feel. Slightly coy, strangely humorous and with the small, placid, stooping dog by his feet looking like a distant relative of the one on the old HMV label.

Young's ability to cheat time in artistic terms is one of his abiding gifts, one that explains why his music still has such power over succeeding musical generations: this is, after all, a 1960s longhair musician who has embraced and applauded disco, punk and, much later, the Seattle grunge sound. Everybody Knows This Is Nowhere was only Young's second solo album, and the first to make any impact at all – although it failed to dent the UK album charts – and yet is it any worse than Tonight's The Night, Freedom or Sleeps With Angels? Artistic achievement is supposed to be an upward curve: Dickens and Shakespeare are the models, but then they both died relatively young. If rock music is a young man's game then Cinnamon Girl conjures up an enormous feeling of joyfulness and optimism, even given the background of the recording, coming as it did after a painful split with Buffalo Springfield and a quick dash to Frank Sinatra's label, Reprise, with Young crying, 'I couldn't get off Atlantic fast enough'.

Not only did the album introduce the world to Crazy Horse, but Cinnamon Girl is the earliest and still the most effective example of Young's playing with D modal tuning, an effect which he says he first used in tandem with Stephen Stills on the Buffalo Springfield circuit. The sound is produced by lifting up a finger on the string in a conventional chord shape and 'letting it just ring'. It was an open-ended effect much influenced by the then-fashionable ragas of Ravi Shankar. (Shankar wasn't always so sensitively appreciated by the West. During one American concert, after the audience had burst into early, spontaneous applause he told them: 'Thank you. As you liked the tuning-up so much you will really love it when I actually start playing.') Ragas employ a modal pattern in which the music rises and falls in a series of tonal shifts, a similar pattern to the more advanced soloings of John Coltrane (a jazz artist much admired by Neil), and is consummated by a guitar break played on two strings but consisting of only one note. There is none of Coltrane's (un)melodic ambition on Cinnamon Girl, the sound is the thing, a churning, droning guitar bursting into rapture during its middle-break solo spot, a wickedly descending bass line and Molina's garage-style drumming.

The words have been described as 'hippy trippy' but Young's insistency cuts across the limply romantic sentiments while the linking verse is reminiscent not only of Eddie Cochran's teen angst anthem, Summertime Blues, but an early nod perhaps in the direction of what Elliot Roberts called his 'strange acquisitiveness'. Young's record deal with Reprise was negotiated for a specific sum; $17,000, the exact amount he needed to buy the house in Topanga Canyon where he was living at the time of this album's release. NY

DOWN BY THE RIVER

First released: Everybody Knows This Is Nowhere (Reprise) **May 1969**

Quite possibly Young's all-time show-stopper, an example of his ability to play slow and yet build up an extraordinary head of steam from a song with a simple melody and a simpler storyline. Young admitted in later years that the song is about violence as well as 'blowing your thing with a chick' – a seemingly unnecessary add-on given the somewhat giveaway chorus, *'Down by the river/I shot my baby'.*

The track, which closed the first side of the album and was one of three written on the day when Young was suffering from a bug, was not to everyone's musical tastes at the time: Bruce Miroff's album review in *Rolling Stone* omitted to mention the song at all, reserving his biggest enthusiasm for the second side's answer to Down By The River, Cowgirl In The Sand, on which he suggested, 'everything works. The lyrics are quietly accusative, while the lead guitar, alternately soaring, piercing and driving, keeps the song surging forward.' Miroff went on to praise 'the peculiar depths of Young's voice', but then Down By The River has always demonstrated the urgency and pleading of his vocalizations. The song was one of the first from Young's own catalogue to be both an instant live hit and a cherished climactic moment at concerts well into the present decade. Not only did Crosby, Stills, Nash And Young use it often as a show-closer but the song was a big feature of gigs by the International Harvesters and on Young's 1993 World Tour with Booker T And The MGs. From 'Frisco to Finsbury Park, Young, ably assisted by Steve Cropper, his own step-sister Astrid on backing vocals, Jim Keltner on drums and Booker T's insistently wailing and throbbing organ work, gave the song the epic treatment it's always merited. It's also clear that by then he'd come to recognize the murderous side to the song, that it was about mental disturbance leading to jealous retribution. Young said, a decade and a half after the song was first recorded: 'He let the dark side come through a little too bright. One afternoon, he took a little stroll down through the field into the forest so that he could hear the water running along there. And he met this woman down there and he told her ... he reached down into his pocket and pulled a little revolver out...'

Young has often said that his opinions about anything may change with the weather, certainly during interviews, so it's unlikely that this description, which is no more than the average listener could work out for themselves, is set in stone. Mind you, if he's telling the truth he might have changed his mind since then about his floating opinions, anyway! But Down By The River does have a feel which is also folksy and countrified, dealing with the well-worked themes of sexual insecurity and climaxing by the riverside – the setting for so many songs of ruin and longing from Clementine (an early Young musical favourite), to Black Is The Colour, the traditional song made popular by Irish folk artist Christy Moore, and The Band's riverboat-gambling Evangelene. The river is a giant theme in American literature and music, not merely the physical and historical presence but the idea of literally passing into a different state of being. By shooting his girl, the protagonist of Young's song has effectively 'crossed over', jumped in himself.

A personal note: at the Finsbury Park gig in July, 1993, a girlfriend and I found ourselves

standing in front of two classic representatives of the rock biz community (journos, PRs, A&R, dealers?) who proceeded to talk throughout the entire set, one of the few to actually make apt use of the arena's thin, tremulous acoustics, from Southern Man through Powderfinger, an exquisite, unrecorded Separate Ways, to a heart-wrenching version of Otis Redding and Cropper's soul classic Dock Of The Bay. Just before I'd decided to whack these mothers, Young broke into the opening chords of Down By The River: the scene had changed utterly, the voice was imploring and tortured, made even more so by the high, whispering vocal accompaniments of Astrid and Annie Stocking. Young's guitar kept coming back, like a dog to a rat, shaking and swerving and juddering, hammering the strings or fizzing with sustain and feedback to say more about the subject than a whole anthology of murder cases from the Newgate Calendar. And the two guys shut up. I actually think their mouths were gaping open. NY

HELPLESS

First released: Deja Vu with Crosby, Stills And Nash (Atlantic) **March 1970**

God, this is a real bastard. I am dreading this entry, but, then again, it's a key to this book, which is neither a biography nor an 'objective' critical study. This is the stark, simple, almost unaccompanied song that Neil Young apparently played to David Crosby, Steven Stills and Graham Nash which so wowed them that Crosby later said something to the effect that they were keen to join Young's band rather than vice versa. Young's involvement with this harmonically gorgeous trio was a key factor in his career: Deja Vu was without doubt one of the most successful interludes of his long career. I will consider it under the entry entitled Ohio. Helpless is a song that he played, drunk and with a clearly visible wedge of cocaine shoved up his nose, at The Band's immortal 'farewell' concert in 1976, when Neil looked so all-out zonked that it seemed that his eyeballs would hit Martin Scorsese's camera lens, recording the whole wasted, San Francisco gig for celluloid posterity.

To many others, Neil's song is a fine, balladic tribute to his childhood, an absurdly idyllic vision of snow and self-entertainment, of fishing and skiing and tobogganning and self-improvement in a very small town in North Ontario, Onemee (pop. 750), before the break-up of his parents' marriage and the move worldwards. But to me, this song, which Neil loves so much that he plays it continuously into the 1990s, even if he gets obsessive about the right key and occasionally squabbles with his musicians, is about Death. It's the song that I played first and independently after the deaths of my parents, within four months of each other, both aged 83, after well over 50 years of marriage. Their commitment was something that neither Neil nor his parents, or indeed I, came close to sharing. Their life, one of simple if not uncomplex adherence to the Christian virtues of faith, hope and love, awed me, in a similar way to the great majesty of this song, which is awed, like so much western art, by the power of Nature. This is not the benign Nature of so many of Young's other songs, not Mother Earth or Country Home or Harvest, where Nature is the force for resurgence and renewal. It is the Nature of Thomas Hardy's *Jude The Obscure* or *Return Of The Native*, or *King Lear,* where us poor humans are 'to the gods as flies to wanton boys. They kill us for their sport.' In 1964, as a sixth-former, I saw the play that first got me interested in the theatre as much as anything outside Shakespeare or Lionel Bart's *Oliver*: Peter Weiss's *The Persecution And Assassination Of Marat As Performed By The Inmates Of The Asylum Of Charenton Under The Direction Of The Marquis De Sade*. It was directed by Peter Brook for the Royal Shakespeare Company and was generally known by its abbreviated title, *Marat/Sade.* Bernard Levin cracked the great joke: 'Have you seen the *Marat/Sade*?' 'No, but I've read the title.'

Brook's production is so close to the spirit of the 1960s: dealing with the dialectic of personal against collective liberation, Marat's revolution versus de Sade's excess. De Sade in Weiss's imagination (and Adrian Mitchell's brilliant verse adaptation) hates Nature: 'Every death, even the cruellest of deaths/drowns in the total indifference of nature/Nature herself would watch unmoved/If we destroyed the entire human race./I hate Nature/This passionless spectator, this unbreakable iceberg face/ that can bear anything.'

This is so close to my own take on Helpless, on those *'big birds flying across the sky'*, on those *'blue, blue windows behind the stars'* which reflect – what? – nothing. It's a song that aches of the wide, vast spaces of northern Canada, spaces that, musically, Neil was to leave bare in his later, best work, so that amid all the volume and feedback, intelligence could reign. But the emptiness of Helpless is about *'chains locked across the doors'*, about our own, very real limitations.

I'm grateful to my colleague at *Time Out*, Peter Paphides, very much the Oscar Wilde of his own pop generation, who says that when he thinks of the line about big birds flying across the sky, he is always reminded of Big Bird from Sesame Street. He can even defend it grammatically: 'Big Bird's flying across the sky'. Maybe he just doesn't want to let it bring me down. I'm sure Neil would have liked both interpretations... NY

AFTER THE GOLDRUSH

First released: After The Goldrush (Reprise) **August 1970**

Though the later Harvest turned out to be Young's most immediately successful album, it's hard to think of a more musically catholic and timelessly bracing recording than the one with which Neil and his collaborators both welcomed in the 1970s, his most productive decade, while simultaneously closing the tin-lid on the 1960s.

After The Goldrush was the second track on the album and its title. Apt as well: each generation makes claims for its own times but, just as David Crosby once said that The Byrds, 'like the Grateful Dead', were 'a magic band', so the 1960s, like the 1930s, was a 'golden decade', a 'goldrush' of ideas, gestures, insanities, changes, postures.

What makes After The Goldrush so exceptionally good an album is its sheer variety: both emotionally and stylistically, even in terms of recording technology. It's a recording that has Young's collaborator Jack Nitzche pasted on it, although Nitzche only played piano on the rapturous When You Dance I Can Really Love, which, like the earlier, unincluded, Winterlong, has traces of Nitzche's earlier producing work in the Phil Spector wall-of-sound mode (which saw its finest flowering in the Crystals' mega-hit Da Doo Ron Ron). Of course, it's also the track most reminiscent of Young's favourite band at the time, and the one he saw as the prototype for Crazy Horse, The Rolling Stones.

It's also a tribute to and a pragmatic recreation of the kind of simple, one-take studio techniques so familiar to Young from adolescent sessions listening to Elvis Presley's Sun recordings, Ricky Nelson's Hello Mary Lou, Goodbye Heart, the two-point rough-diamond harmonies of the Everly Brothers, the wailful Gene Pitney and, most influentially, Roy Orbison. There is a staggeringly bizarre coincidence here which shows how art and life have a funny way of imitating each other. It's the stuff of rock legend that this album was a redundant soundtrack written for Young's neighbour and movie-actor friend Dean Stockwell, at a time when Young and his girlfriend (later wife), Susan Acevedo, had started getting interested in home movies big-time. Like Carl Hiaasen's novel about the hurricane season in Florida, *Stormy Weather*, the movie was supposed to show the effects of a huge tidal wave on the residents of Topanga and district.

While only the title track and perhaps the London-written Don't Let it Bring You Down would seem to have any relevance to such a project, Birds, undoubtedly one of Young's finest and most undervalued love songs, is so much a homage to Orbison's doleful, confessional singing style that it even borrows the clinching statement 'It's over,' itself, of course, the title of an Orbison song. Now, here's the tie-in: Stockwell, who was born in 1936, was a successful child actor before making his biggest impact as the DH Lawrence character in Jack Cardiff's 1960 film of *Sons And Lovers*. Given his assortment of roles in a lot of very topical dreamy, trippy films like Dennis Hopper's *The Last Movie*, it's little wonder that this North Hollywood showbiz native became friendly with Neil, but it's the cementing of the Orbison connection that gives most room for pause. After a fallow period in the late 1970s, Stockwell not only emerged to co-direct with Young his 1982 film, *Human Highway*, but in 1986 made an outstanding cult-generating appearance as a terrifying, androgynous badass colleague of

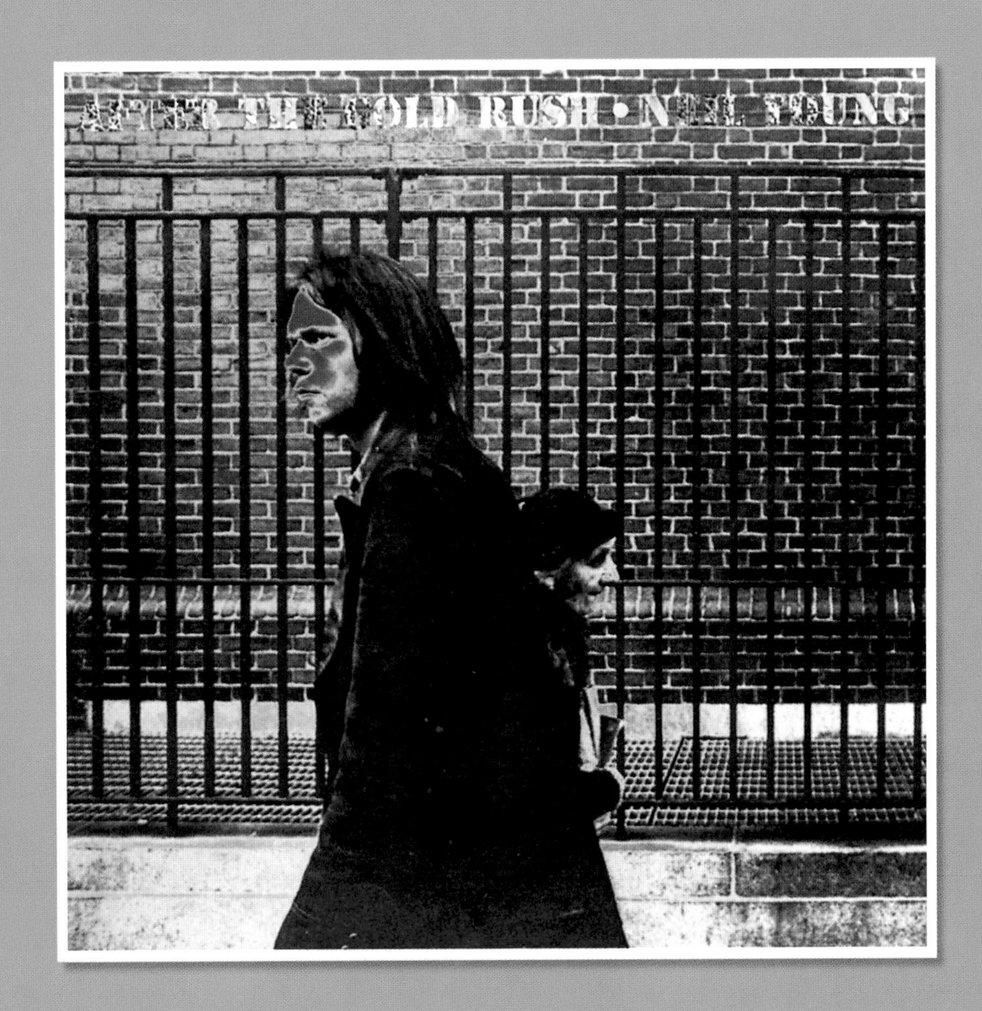
AFTER THE GOLD RUSH • NEIL YOUNG

Dennis Hopper's in David Lynch's classic movie, *Blue Velvet*. And what does Dean's torch-singer Ben do the most frightening, teeth-marks-on-the-door-handle version of? Why, Roy Orbison's In Dreams (well, it's close!).

This simple sentence, 'It's over,' which carries with it the finality almost of *King Lear's* awful repetitions of 'Nothing' and 'Never', is the personal-relationships coda to Jim Morrison's more politically-twisted The End, with its more obviously generalized concerns of the period, later reflected, of course, by the fantastic noiseless bombing sequence that opens Francis Ford Coppola's *Apocalypse Now*. By this time, Young's position as the fourth leg of the much-vaunted, nay, 'American-Beatles'-touted Crosby, Stills, Nash And Young had not only raised his profile enormously (and his blood-pressure, being back on the guitar-and-ego front line with Stills), but had forced him to confront the political demons around at this time, most brilliantly with Ohio, but also with Southern Man. But, as Young made it clear in one particularly revealing interview in *Rolling Stone* with Elliot Blinder, he wasn't really interested in revolution. In an exchange with some representatives from RAW (Right-A-Wrong) seeking to legalize marijuana, Young had seemed to distance himself in a way not unreminiscent of The Beatles on every take of Revolution bar the ghastly Number 9: *'If you go carrying pictures of Chairman Mao, you ain't gonna make it with anyone, anyhow.'* So Young talks of a possible 'very violent revolution' in terms obviously distant: 'Yeah, I'll get a big cannon if they're gonna have a revolution. I'll sit up on top of my studio there, with my material gains after the game, and, uh, contemplate my future...' No wonder After The Goldrush is so memorable for the vulnerability and elegance of love songs like Birds, Only

Love Can Break Your Heart and I Believe In You; no wonder its politics are constantly subsumed by its musicality: the melodic and harmonic clashes of pianos (Nitzche, Young and Nils Lofgren), guitars both distorted and pellucidly acoustic, the harmonies of Stills, the temporarily back-in-favour junk-obsessed Danny Whitten, the precocious Nils Lofgren and Molina, and Young's never-finer harmonica overlicks.

Lyrically, After The Goldrush itself is one of Young's most interesting songs to date, but the vocal is a dog, an early example of Young's dangerous inability to find a suitable register for his limited voice. Sung in D instead of the more suitable C, the real problem occurs when the shift from A to B minor comes, as in *'There was a fanfare blowing'* and *'There was a band playing'*, which are surely embarrassing places to start losing it musically. But as well as the churchy, hymn-like directness of Young's piano, the lyric writing has a structured, Ancient And Modern quality to it: three verses with the last line repeated dolefully, and a burst of brass (a mute-trumpet or French horn perhaps, fuzzy shades of For No One off Revolver?) instead of Young's often rapturous harmonica in later live performances.

Each stanza is a snapshot of history: a medieval scene of such splendour and pageantry that only a LA resident could have invented it, climaxing with the wonderful if physically absurd image of an archer splitting a tree with an arrow. The song's bittersweet core, a bleakly contemporary picture of a man sitting in *'a burned-out basement'* (Goldrush was almost wholly made in the basement studio of Young's all-wood Topanga home) feeling like getting 'high', which could be 'stoned' or just 'happy' and: *'Thinking about what a friend had said/I was hoping it was a lie.'* Always introspective, certainly by the dippily excessive standards of the time and place, Young has created a magnificent monosyllabic take on the paranoia, both group and individual, of the day. It's akin to Robert Burns' oft-quoted remarks about having the gift to see ourselves as others see us, and an awesomely economical creation of all those druggy, bitchy, extended-family conversations that folks would have over herb teas and brownies at Our House.

I don't like the escapist cop-out of the final verse, although its apocalyptic vision was shared by CSN&Y's Wooden Ships, featured on the Woodstock album and also once mooted as a possible screenplay. Leaving the planet for a new home in the sun reflects what turned out to be accurate environmental concerns (Young now changes the last two words of *'look at mother nature on the run in the nineteen-seventies'* to *'twentieth century'*). But its escapism reminds me of that other politically reluctant artist from a much earlier period, John Osborne, whose angry young protagonist in the groundbreaking *Look Back In Anger* turns his back on the real world to play bunny-hunting with his upper-class, ironing-board-bound wife. No wonder Young at the time expressed so much rapture at the stories in the *National Enquirer* of space travellers who were here in prehistoric days, and so on. He may have been poignantly aware of the fragility of human relationships but Abbie Hoffman or Dave Spart he certainly wasn't, and isn't... NY

DON'T LET IT BRING YOU DOWN

First released: After The Goldrush (Reprise) **August 1970**

One of Young's quirkier, more indirect ballads, this has an urgency and a churn to it that separates it from the more love-taken songs of this period. A perennial crowd-pleaser, it's another example of Young's open-tuning technique, which allows easy access to a variety of chord changes without recourse to elaborate finger-work on the frets. Oddly, it was actually written in London during a January tour by Crosby, Stills, Nash And Young that led them to the Albert Hall and a star-studded audience which included Paul McCartney and popular folkies Julie Felix and Donovan. Stephen Stills admitted to *Melody Maker* that the band felt 'somehow as if we were on trial' and indicated a first-time feeling of nerves, which was somewhat strange given the immortalized outburst at the start of their Woodstock set earlier in August 1969: 'This is only the second time we've played together. Man, we're scared shitless.'

The London setting is hinted at by the very English 'lorries' which roll by as an old man is *'lying by the side of the road'* and *'the morning paper flies'*. It's not necessarily a 'placed' song, though, especially with the more recognisably American imagery of moaning sirens and a *'blue moon sinking from the weight of the load'*. It's an eerie piece, a feeling that Neil capitalized upon in later years when he started to perform it in a lower, deeper key. Despite its graphic and sometimes violent overview, peaking with the *'white cane lying in the gutter in the lane'*, it's the chorus that really makes this song. Freudian analysis connects burning buildings, particularly buildings of great majesty like towers, palaces or castles, with the experience of breaking up, of abandoning relationships, literally 'turning'. If you find someone who's 'turning' then you will 'come around'. It's a classic example of Neil's lyrical playfulness, which encompasses both the physical act of two people meeting at the right time, and the idea of finding emotional solace in something new, of literally being woken up, coming around.

Annie Lennox recorded a particularly fine version of this song on her 1995 solo album, Medusa; orchestrated and far more operatic than the original but highlighting its full musical potential. Despite the fragmentary nature of the writing, the concern with inner-city deprivation would resurface much later in Young's career-turning album Freedom from 1989, notably in the almost film noir blitzkrieg of Crime In The City (Sixty To Zero Part 1). NY

SOUTHERN MAN

First released: After The Goldrush **August 1970**

Another example of the variety and range of After The Goldrush, Southern Man is a song that Young still performs live at full volume and which was a climactic moment on the Crazy Horse tours of two decades ago. As a political song it seems to have been overrated: given that the author was a Canadian who lived in relatively progressive multi-racial Los Angeles, it is a song which is devoid of much direct experience of racism, the images not only antique and even ante-bellum but strangely second-hand. It's as if *Mandingo* meets *Uncle Tom's Cabin* and *In The Heat Of The Night*. Young could be accused of a bit of exploitation as well, with his almost to-order reprise of the song on Harvest, Alabama, although both tunes at least have arresting hand-picked solo guitar intros. Makes you wonder if Young wasn't planning to go through the entire Confederacy: Damn You Arkansas, Tennessee, and West Virginia, Where Were You? have so far not surfaced. Mind you, it's another great tribute to Young's quirky and often generous sense of humour and lack of self-importance that when Southern men Lynyrd Skynyrd took umbrage and wrote Sweet Home Alabama in response in 1974, Neil went out of his way to say how much he preferred it to his own song(s). Indeed, poignantly, two weeks after three members of Lynyrd Skynyrd perished in an air crash, Young performed a version of their song at a birthday concert and dedicated to 'a couple of friends in the sky'. He was most pleased of all to get an actual name-check, even if it was followed by a question about his conscience, personal or political or both.

The image of the South in the 1960s can't have been that much different for those of us growing up in Britain. We too were bombarded with images from the civil rights campaigns: attempts to get blacks to register to vote; to attend hitherto segregated schools and universities; to eat in white diners and sit in seats reserved for whites on the buses; the so-called freedom riders. There were vivid newsreels showing black protesters flattened by police water cannon, savaged by attack dogs in Birmingham, Alabama, beaten up by Joe and Jolene Public on the sidewalks and pavements of Mississippi and Arkansas. It was easy to get self-righteous, and only maturity and a visit to the haunted, beautiful and ultra-polite South can add complexity and humanity to one's own morally blinkered view. The great American novelist Richard Ford, born in Jackson, Mississippi, across the way from great writers like William Faulkner and Eudora Welty, told me about the experience: 'When James Meredith became the first black man to register at the University of Mississippi, a crowd of my high school friends went along to holler. Medger Evers was murdered in Jackson. There were many brave people around at that time, freedom riders, activists, people from the North, white and black, who were beaten, even murdered for the cause. My own decision was simply to get out, to leave as soon as I could, to breathe fresh air.' Then he added, intriguingly: 'When I lived in the South I was considered as something of a liberal; as soon as I went to college in Michigan I was seen as this redneck.'

There's one arresting stanza to Southern Man, after all the clichés about plantations and shacks, mansions, bullwhips and burning crosses. Young adds a whole new dimension, rather as Shakespeare makes his words more real when he conjures up imagery from the stage, by

making himself the protagonist of the song's bigotry. As well as slagging off the Louisa May Alcott-style Lillie Bell, for (presumably) making (or thinking about making) the beast with two backs with a black man, Neil's voice hammers home the threat *'Swear by God I'm gonna cut him down.'* This is a tight, nasty use of words, which could mean literally to kill or, even more horrible, to castrate. Castration was as much a feature of Ku Klux Klan activity as lynching and cross-burning, and William Bradford Huie's superb *Three Lives For Mississippi*, the book that inspired the much later film, *Mississippi Burning*, details one such deeply horrific incident where a terrified black man had to watch helplessly as his testicles were razor-bladed into a plastic cup.

The playing on this track is splendid, the garage-style spontaneity and directness emphasized by the way in which the track seems to start in the middle of some jam, with Lofgren's piano keeping basic rattling time (Lofgren was asked to play piano on these sessions and agreed only after finding that the right hand was the same as for his accordion!). Young's guitar work is raw, urgent, controlled and forever switching tone, at one point playing the same note over and over like some zonked-out embittered version of Carlos Santana, sounding, as David Downing writes wonderfully, 'like an assassin sending redundant bullets into a corpse'. Unfortunately, at the time *Rolling Stone*'s Langdon Winner didn't agree, finding the ensemble playing on Southern Man 'sloppy and disconnected': 'The piano, bass and drums search for each other like lovers lost in the sand dunes, but although they see each other's footprints now and then, they never really come together.' Pass the sick bag, Lillie Bell.

As polemics go, Southern Man isn't a patch on his mentor Dylan's much earlier Highway 61 Revisited, with its powerful, poetically complex series of oblique images as ambiguous as any poem chosen by William Empson for his classic study of multiple-meaning, *Seven Types Of Ambiguity*: *'God said to Abraham kill me a son'* ushers in a masterpiece which, compared with Southern Man and Alabama, is Tennessee Williams to Young's daytime soaps. NY

OUT ON A WEEKEND & HEART OF GOLD

First released: Harvest (Reprise) **February 1972**

A double entry here for two songs with a degree of similarity which are tracks one and four of the album that was to transform Young's career and reputation in the wider pop world to a degree that is both remarkable and, to him, something of a poisoned chalice. The album topped the charts on both sides of the Atlantic and in Heart Of Gold produced Young's only real chart hit – and what a hit it was, reaching number one in America and scraping the top ten in Britain. In the early 1970s, everyone who had long hair, a long dress, a kaftan, a chillum, a pestle and mortar, a tie-dyed teeshirt, a Christopher Logue poster over their bed, a copy of *The Tibetan Book Of The Dead* or Richard Neville's pleasure bible, *Play Power*, listened to this album either alone or in company. And thought mostly good thoughts, even after reading the bit in Neville's book about a woman who opinedthat rock bands should be drug-tested before they went on stage, in the manner of footballers and other athletes.

These tracks, as well as being two of the catchiest, tuneful and well-produced songs of his entire career, also sum up the perceived spirit of the album, which is one of slightly blissful, easy-paced countrified rock sometimes at odds with the sad-young-white-boy ennui of some of the lyrics, again exemplified by both these songs with their sorta-up-but-sorta-down sentiments. Despite, or maybe because of, its commercial success, the album was clobbered by some critics, notably *Rolling Stone*, who decried its so-called parade of LA superstar clichés and, in his own unfathomable way, by Young himself, who on his grunge days manages to make a word like 'finest' sound like the worst insult in the world and who memorably accused its success of driving him 'into the middle of the road'. But then when it comes to looking gift horses in the mouth, Young can give Lester Piggott on a stepladder a run for his money.

The whole story of Harvest is another case of the happy accidents which so affect art and the artist. (Orson Welles was critically acclaimed for a Turkish bath scene filmed in the nude for his *Othello* because the company had no costumes; writer Roddy Doyle was desperate to end his controversial television drama series, *Family*, with a domestic rendition of Always Look On The Bright Side Of Life until producer Andrew Eaton, among others, persuaded him to change it to the Lord's Prayer. Naturally, Doyle got all the credit. Etcetera.)

The album does contain both lavishly orchestrated numbers (the ludicrously overstated There's A World stretched the talents of the London Symphony Orchestra) and some hard rocking, notably on Words and Alabama, two of three tracks that were added after the main sessions. But its more successful tunefulness, its quiet broodiness, and the wonderful tone of these two tracks which sound almost buskery in a one-man-band, saucepan-lid-on-the-knees and a song-in-my-heart kinda way, is wholly down to the fact that Young recorded most of it in severe pain from a crippling back injury received when he spasmed while carrying a slab of polished walnut. He could only stand for around four hours a day, took forty-five minutes to stumble with the solicitous David Crosby from his home to the recording studio a quarter of a mile away, and was in and out of hospital for two years – which added a touching medical soap opera gloss to his romance at the time with actress Carrie Snodgress, who he'd fancied after seeing her in the unpromisingly-titled Frank Perry movie, *Diary of A Mad Housewife*.

ON BROWNE

Young had suffered back trouble intermittently since his bout of polio as a child, an illness that had left him weaker on one side and had caused his muscles and several discs to eventually give way and cause him to seek major medical help. I have to say that Young's failure to make much out of this period in interviews is a sign of genuine nobility: anyone who has suffered from serious back trouble knows how enervating and depressing it can be; in late 1970 it must have been bleak indeed, given that Young eventually had to have discs removed in procedures which would have undoubtedly entailed some of the more agonizing procedures in medicine, notably the dreaded lumbar puncture, more familiarly known as the 'spinal tap'. Four years later, England football captain Gerry Francis was to call the long back injury which shortened his playing career one of the blackest times of his life, times in which the treatments were sometimes worse than the ailment.

Young says that he spent a lot of time on his back over the next two years, lying there thinking, but his best decision-making process came almost on a prayer: both Heart Of Gold and Out On A Weekend are made by the arrangement, by the over-emphatic bass, the keening underpinning of Ben Keith's harmonica-tuned steel and pedal steel guitars, and the throbbing, thudding heart of Kenny Buttrey's slow, purposeful backbeat drumming, recorded to take up an appealingly forward-stage position in the overall sound of the songs. The trio, completed by Nashville session bassist Tim Drummond, were dubbed The Stray Gators, and were well complemented by Jack Nitzche on piano, Linda Ronstadt, who provided the backing vocal at the end of Heart Of Gold, Young's big rival in the lovelorn folk-rock warbler stakes, James Taylor, and even charming vocal touches by Crosby, Stills and Nash.

On Out On A Weekend, Young's harmonica intro has never been more charismatic, more what-the-fuck-is-that? appealing, and, as in Heart Of Gold, it makes such a naked contribution to the melody that it is unsurprising that Young wanted Keith's floating country contributions to add colour to what he was doing. As songs, both are deceptively subtle: Out On A Weekend talks of depression, longing and rootlessness in a way that sounds more appealing than that description because of the stark, monosyllabic soundbite with which it begins: *'Think I'll pack it in and buy a pick-up/Take it down to LA.'* Which is, after all, give or take a few vehicle changes, what he did. It's also a song which, despite oozing ennui, offers the closing prospect of a man on the edge of a *'brand new day'* who is happy beyond the point of words, who *'tries to speak but can't begin to say'*; just as complete joy or self-realization is supposed to be one step ahead of language, just as, in Walter Pater's oft-used phrase, 'All art aspires to the condition of music.'

Heart Of Gold is the song that all non-Young aficionados would name if asked to do a Neil word association test. Young's biographer David Downing said it was, 'what puppies would sound like if they were set to music', which is witty but misses what to me is an edge that undercuts the song's musical cheeriness. It's also a concise piece of autobiography, as well as retreading an age-old and universal theme about the difference between real and false value. Oscar Wilde said that a cynic is a man who knows the price of everything and the value of nothing: so Heart Of Gold is a quest song conjuring up references to both a personal Holy Grail of contentment and stability and the goldrush of his journey from Canada to Los Angeles to find the 24-carat lode of fame and fortune.

On that quest, Young has freely admitted he could be ruthless, ditching friends and collaborators when and where he had to, even bitching at Crosby, Stills and Nash for using him as a glorified electric guitarist, without fully acknowledging the undoubted influence they were to have on his own music. *'I've been to Hollywood, I've been to Redwood/I've crossed the ocean for a heart of gold.'* Young had done all this: sampled the sleaze of Tinseltown, indulged his love of the countryside and nature and been to Europe. In 1932, Mae West, famous for replying to a reporter who asked her how she held her liquor, 'by the ears', boasted famously: 'I'm not a little girl from a little town makin' good in a big town. I'm a big girl from a big town makin' good in a little town.' But then few found Hollywood so easy to handle and it's certain that Young, with his bad back and his penchant for introspection, wasn't one of them. With Harvest he found not so much a heart of gold as a mountain of it, even using it to finance his first live concert movie, *Journey Through The Past*, in late 1972, a movie which was never released in Britain because of its depiction of a junkie shooting up.

On the personal front, Young's romance with Snodgress soon blossomed, although by this time he'd already had one failed marriage, to restaurant manageress Susan Acevedo, whose decorative, domesticated manners and blonde, long-haired good looks were very much the template at the time for rock 'chicks'. Hence, perhaps, the truly dreadful, desperately orchestral A Man Needs A Maid, which is every bit as crummy as its title suggests despite later apologists who have tried to suggest that Young was merely trying to look for clear lines of conduct in his personal relationships.

So why 'maid', with its wimpy blend of archaic servitude and sexual purity? Why not A Man Needs A Lady Plumber or A Man Needs A Female Cop? At this time, sexual politics was in its infancy, not least among self-regarding southern Californian rock musicians. Although the frocks were prettier and the cakes and pastries more tasty, the 'maids' of Topanga and Laurel Canyons hadn't advanced much from the political position held by the character in Brecht's Caucasian Chalk Circle who avers that women are good for only two things: in the kitchen and opening their legs. NY

Harvest
Neil Young

THE NEEDLE AND THE DAMAGE DONE

First released: Harvest (Reprise) **February 1972**

Given that Neil Young makes quirky, personal choices from his back catalogue in live performance, this must either be one of his favourites or, put cynically, an easy crowd-pleaser. Slow and folky with a blues edge, it begins promisingly enough with an intro reminiscent of Robert Johnson's Won't You Come Into My Kitchen, or The Rolling Stones' Sister Morphine. This is a song about enticement, hence the upfront *'I caught you knocking at my cellar door/I love you baby/Can I have some more?'*

Heroin. It's a song that was inspired by Crazy Horse guitarist Danny Whitten's early descent into junkiedom, but it's also a song ruined by the sentimental image at the end. *'But every junkie's like a setting sun'* gets easy applause and yet seems preposterously inapt. Around this time, I was crashing near Brian Jones' home in London with a friend who had a houseful of junkies. They stole everything, even the lightbulbs. I got so paranoid I slept with my suitcase under the mattress. One morning very early I awoke to find a girl trying to pull the suitcase out from under me. When I looked into her face it wasn't full of remorse or even a trace of guilt, just sheer, hateful irritation.

This is junk, this is the world that Irvine Welsh's *Trainspotting* and William Burroughs' *Junkie* opened up to us; that's not to say that junkies are animals, just that their habit makes them behave like animals, but with a lot more guile. Of course, Young was to return to addiction in the wake of Whitten and Bruce Berry's deaths with the recording of the infinitely more challenging, less wimpified Tonight's The Night. But the song lives on: on the highly-acclaimed Unplugged, on live gigs from Amsterdam to Hong Kong. And people still cheer. NY

OHIO

First released: So Far with Crosby, Stills And Nash (Atlantic) **July 1974**

Finally albumized on Crosby, Stills, Nash And Young's chart-topping So Far four years after its release as a single and the tragic events which inspired it, Ohio represents the most splendid moment in Neil Young's sometimes fraught relationship with CS&N. Young, speaking in 1977, three years after the album's release to coincide with a last, sensational world tour by the outfit, said: 'It's hard to believe that I had to write this song. Ironic that I had to capitalize on the deaths of those students.'

When Young refers to having to write this song, he's being more accurate than might at first seem apparent. Johnny Rogan, who is usually right about these things, believes that the song is of greater importance to the more politicized David Crosby, who virtually force-fed Young the *Time* magazine article which detailed the killings by National Guardsmen of four students at Kent State University, Ohio, during a crazed summer of protests against the war in Vietnam and its expansion into Cambodia. Rogan tells me not only that Crosby, Stills and Nash have performed the song more times than Young ever has, but that Neil even failed to show for a reunion concert at Kent State in 1997.

That said, Young did write it, in roughly fifteen minutes, and in common with so much cut-up, agitprop, reportage culture of this heady time, it makes a powerful fist of distilling 10,000 words of complex, first-rate journalism into a few soundbites of delicious rage and pity. *'This summer I hear the drumming/Four dead in Ohio.'* The poster-art nature of the whole process is underlined by the amazing speed with which the single appeared, ten days after Young recorded it in Pescadero, California, with Steven Stills' Find The Cost Of Freedom on the B-side; the whole event couldn't have happened without the help of Atlantic boss Ahmet Ertegun, who got the tapes on a plane to New York, and without CSN&Y's enormous clout with the record company. The single, which was released with much less impact in the UK in August, soon reached number 14 in the US charts. This recording happened on 21 May 1970, only days after the 18 May issue of *Time* which headlined ten pages of news and photos: 'THE NATION: At War With War.'

By the time the article appeared, no less than 441 colleges and universities had been affected to the point of shutdown by the events in Ohio, which themselves have all the bloody irony and absurdity of the Charge of the Light Brigade. A riot, which ended in death on the Monday, began in lighthearted fashion the Friday before as students, drunk on booze and rock music, began to throw stones and chant anti-war slogans in the street. After a rally aimed in part at forcing a rise in black student admissions by 5,000, war protesters managed to hijack the mood of about 800 people in attendance. Without consultation with the university, state governor James Rhodes had around 500 National Guardsmen sent to the campus, armed with M-1 semi-automatics, tear gas and pistols. The guardsmen were tired and despite initial bouts of hobnobbing with college hippies eventually hostile and confused. The shooting started after a group of guardsmen without a leader became trapped at the top of a hill where they were being pelted with rocks and other missiles. Eyewitnesses claimed that 'an officer brought his baton down in a sweeping signal' according to *Time*, while a college professor shouted famously: 'They are shooting blanks – they are shooting blanks!' 'My God, they're killing us!' one terrified girl screamed out. As well as the four who were killed, ten students were injured, three seriously and one so badly that he was paralysed below the waist. Inevitably, none of the dead were leaders or even notably radical: one of the slain, Alison Krause, a 19-year-old pacifist who studied art history, had placed a flower in a guardsman's rifle barrel and whispered, 'Flowers are better than bullets.' Her father asked feelingly: 'Is dissent a crime? Is this a reason for killing her?' And the tenor of the report was even more powerful for its well-practised objectivity and restraint: 'A river of blood ran from the head of one boy, saturating his school books. One youth held a cloth against the abdomen of another, futilely trying to check the bleeding.' *'What if you knew her, and saw her dead on the ground?/How can you run when you know?'*

This was America at war with itself, with its own children: the pride that had staunched the tears of those white middle-class parents in the mid-1960s as they buried their murdered civil rights activist children had given way by the end of the decade to a feeling of bewilderment and even alienation. There was a perfect contemporary illustration of this in John G Alvidsen's now neglected film, *Joe*, which was released in the year of Kent State: Joe, played by Peter Boyle, is a construction worker, a hard-hat Joe who meets a businessman in a bar who has just shot his daughter's drug addict lover. The two become united by their hatred of hippies, and the film ends tragically when the businessman tracks his own daughter down to a remote rural commune and shoots her in the back by accident. It's a crude film by a director who went on to make *Rocky*, but its concerns mirror the time just as much as Richard Nixon's own futile attempts to communicate with peace marchers in Washington shortly after the Kent State massacre. Nixon's remarks about college football and Neville Chamberlain and Winston Churchill met with bewilderment on the steps of the Lincoln Memorial. 'We're finally on our own.' Or so it suddenly seemed.

Now, of course, the spectre has turned back on the change-it-all 1960s. Note Atom Egoyan's award-winning *The Sweet Hereafter*, filmed in Young's own Canada, and based on Russell Banks' novel about a small town coming to grips with its grief after a school bus crash. Ian Holm's central character, Mitchell Stephens, is a claims lawyer haunted by his alienation from a daughter who is addicted to crack. Hard drugs, unemployment, HIV, The Spice Girls. The generation gap hasn't been closed very much at all.

The decade ended spectacularly badly for America: riots in the streets, the slayings of Robert Kennedy and Martin Luther King; peace and love had given way to Charles Manson, the possibilities of Woodstock to the mayhem and murder of Altamont, where Paul Kantner of Jefferson Airplane took a punch from a drunken Hell's Angel (he got off lightly) and told *Rolling Stone* magazine afterwards that Mick Jagger's problem was that 'his idea of a Hell's Angel is Peter Fonda', referring to the successful road movie, *Easy Rider*, ironically, the film for which Stills originally and unsuccessfully submitted Find The Cost Of Freedom and which again ends with hippy bike-nomads being mown down by a redneck truck driver. When a friend of mine saw the film in San Antonio, Texas, the whole audience stood up and cheered. Ohio is a postcard

from the edge, and certainly a finer, more placed footnote than anything produced in Britain, certainly more than The Rolling Stones' pathetic, unfocused Street Fighting Man.

Of course, there has been much inevitable talk about the place Ohio occupied in the repertoire of a band who quickly became notorious for the bacchanalia of its tours. This was certainly the case on the first major tour in 1970, when drugs and even hookers were in ample supply and the band's attitude to both its catering and stage props must have had some influence on Rob Reiner's *This Is Spinal Tap*, particularly the scene where Tap's Nigel Tufnell professes his inability to 'work' with sandwiches made from thin, small slices of bread. But Ohio endures, whether it be in later performances or the blitzing original on which Young's guitar positively trembles with anger and on which Crosby screams at the dying fall, 'How many more? Why?' – a session in which he collapsed in tears at the end.

Young still performs the song, usually as a solo acoustic number, when the fancy takes him. At a concert in Amsterdam in July 1993, recorded on Dutch radio, Young dedicated the song to 'a little Chinese boy' who stood in front of a tank in Tiananmen Square, Peking. 'You bet the authorities found out who he was. What do you think happened to that Chinese boy?' Whatever may be rightly said about Young's lack of real political engagement, or the hypocrisy of self-styled rock radicals like David Crosby ,who at least had the nerve to produce an awesomely revelatory autobiography in *Long Time Gone*, Ohio remains as a song which both records an event which hardened attitudes, points a finger in the right direction and still finds time to recreate feelings both of bitterness and dread in the band's own constituency of fans. NY

REVOLUTION BLUES

First released: On The Beach (Reprise) **July 1974**

On The Beach is a curious business: it comes before Tonight's The Night the album, but after Tonight's The Night the tour; it is one of half a dozen Young albums as yet unavailable on CD in Britain, but if you can track down a second-hand copy it's well worth the effort. No album sounds better on vinyl. And despite its mixed reviews at the time, one is sorely tempted to agree with Johnny Rogan, who thinks it one of Young's finest ever, certainly the second side on the album which contains just three tracks.

On The Beach is a lament for the 1960s, recalled with the benefit of brooding hindsight. It's about growing up to the point of ageing: the title track is almost a geriatric rerun of Out On A Weekend, with the lonely boy now *'living on the beach/But those seagulls are still out of reach'*. Even the jaunty opener, Walk On, contains lines that my own father could have connected with, being full of nostalgia for nights staying up and having fun, not worried about being broke. Well, maybe not the bit about *'getting crazed'*. While Ambulance Blues, considered later here, begins with the memory *'Back in those old folkie days'* as if he were talking about Before The Flood and not before *Sunset Boulevard*.

Two things elevate it in particular: given that Young was voted the ninth best rock guitarist in history by a poll for *Mojo* magazine, it's extraordinary how little influence blues has had on his playing, certainly much less than the other musicians in that top ten. On The Beach contains three blues, as well as a splendid country rag in For The Turnstile and an earlier, mournfully beautiful ballad, See The Sky About To Rain. But these are less the blues of Robert Johnson or Bukka White than Bob Dylan's urban white blues. Dylan's influence on On The Beach is immense, notably his pulsatingly enraged Bringing It All Back Home: if you put Revolution Blues and Vampire Blues together you can almost hear Dylan's savage Outlaw Blues, while the mordant humour of the lyrics is wholly in keeping with Bob's tone as far back as The Lonesome Death Of Hetty Carroll.

Revolution Blues isn't the best music on this astonishing record, but it is the best example of its other claim to fame. On The Beach is about recent American history and politics, from the newspaper on the sand of the cover (such a deliberately tacky cover), with its headline about Richard Nixon's resignation, to this song, which is powered by direct images of America's worst nightmare: Charles Manson.

Along with Ian Brady and Myra Hindley, Manson was one of the world's most notorious criminals of the decade: he was also a near neighbour of most of LA's rock community, including Young, who had met him socially, if that's the word, and pronounced him 'charismatic'. Manson was a crazed slayer, who kept his devoted Family members hypnotized by a mix of hard hallucinogenics and constant sexual activity, the more degrading the better for Charlie.

Manson was a shaman, a prophet, a leader, a role model for impressionable middle-class kids who'd argued with their parents or just wanted to hit the hippy scene. Like Neil Young, Manson was also very rock 'n' roll, a man who once boasted that he would be 'bigger than the Beatles', a man who befriended Young's associate Dennis Wilson of the Beach Boys. Wilson so fell under Manson's spell that he set up recording sessions at the same studios where most of On The Beach was recorded; Manson 'borrowed' money from Wilson, crashed his car, provided him with willing chicks and was later to so terrorize Wilson, who had a young son, that he vowed never to speak about Manson again. Wilson , who died in 1983, even paid the Manson family's VD clinic tab, which he said was the costliest in the history of the Californian state.

It's no wonder that the rock community, particularly LA's, had such an embarrassed, muted response to Manson's crimes and career: he wanted to be like them but he ended up killing them, despoiling their Hollywood mansions with words he had gleaned illiterately from the Beatles' White Album. I once asked Paul McCartney how he felt when told that Manson had created a whole revolutionary scenario out of his admittedly demonic rocker, Helter Skelter. 'It was awful, we were knocked sideways. We just hid, really, kept our heads down'.

It wasn't just Helter Skelter: Manson, a racist and career criminal who loved to kill humans but pronounced flowers, plants and animals inviolable, saw the most hidden meanings in George Harrison's harmless anti-meat song Piggies, as well as Blackbird, Revolution No.1 and the terrible montage, Revolution No.9, which is the most skipped-over track in CD history and which you have to be insane to still enjoy. What Manson made of the lyrics from Revolution No.1 (*'But if you're looking for money for minds that hate/I tell you brother you're going to have to wait'*) isn't clear.

Revolution Blues climaxes with a chiller-diller lyric involving dune buggies by the million and the evocation of showbusiness celebrities murdered in their cars by someone who hates them, 'worse than lepers'.

This is the apocalypse: after all, Manson's dune buggy-driving family never numbered more than forty; and the reference to cars is clearly a nod to the killing by four gunshots of Steven Parent, in his car, outside the Polanski home. An earlier verse tells: *'Well it's so good to be here asleep on your lawn/Remember your guard dog/Well I'm afraid that he's gone/It was such a drag to hear him/Whining all night long.'* When Leno and Rosemary LaBianca were murdered on a raid led by Manson, the guard dogs watched in silence and licked the hands of the three killers.

Young's whole song, with its image of doves being set free just by a factory that produces 'computer logs', is energetically ambivalent: Young seems to be both potential victim (his friend Terry Melcher, a record producer, was on Manson's celebrity death list) and potential killer. After all, Manson was a Dorian Gray portrait of the kind of desert hippy ethic that so much of the Californian rock scene ostensibly espoused. Was Manson a monster or a martyr? At the time of his arrest, underground paper *Tuesday's Child* called him The Man Of The Year.

Revolution Blues also touches, particularly in its first verse, on the almost equally wacky case of Patty Hearst, the newspaper heiress who was kidnapped in February 1974 by members of the Symbionese Liberation Army. After 57 days of hideous captivity, Hearst emerged transformed into an urban guerrilla. Another disenchanted girl from an unbroken home who got the deadly bug. Intriguing, given the Dylan connection that the line-up on this track includes the Band's Rick Danko and Levon Helm.

Although I once had a crazed, mercifully brief correspondence with one of Manson's Family members, the nearest I came to witnessing that kind of shock wave was in 1985 when I visited Marion Federal Penitentiary in Illinois where double-murderer and author Jack Henry Abbott was serving life without parole in a top-security institution built to replace Alcatraz. Like Manson, Abbott's mother was a prostitute; like Manson, Abbott was in state institutions from childhood; like Manson, Abbott had talent approaching genius, but it was on the page and not in dealing with people and conning young girls. After being released on parole after the acclaim that greeted his book of letters from prison to Norman Mailer, *In The Belly Of The Beast*, Abbott re-offended, killing a man for no reason at all, utterly unprepared for fame and freedom. When Manson was released from jail in 1967, it was against his will. When I spoke with Abbott, he had clearly become deranged, suffering paranoid delusions

that his plight was the result of a Jewish-CIA conspiracy. Most of all, he feared being transferred to a state prison in New York. He would be killed for his celebrity, he said. And he was right. In many ways, Abbott's life was a genuine, profound tragedy; Manson's was more of a bloody farce. NY

AMBULANCE BLUES

First released: On The Beach (Reprise) **July 1974**

Ambulance Blues is worth highlighting, not just for its random use of autobiographical references to Young's Canadian years, notably the lines on Sweet Isabella, named for the street in Toronto where he dossed as a folkie on the club trail. It is also a song that Neil freely and cheerfully admits to having 'copped' from Bert Jansch, the Glasgow-born guitarist who is Young's favourite acoustic performer and who came in at number 42 in the *Mojo* magazine all-time greats chart.

In 1992, Young told *Guitar Player* magazine: 'But as much of a great guitar player as Jimi (Hendrix) was, Bert Jansch is the same thing for acoustic guitar. The very first record that he made – great record. It came from England and I was particularly impressed by Needle Of Death, this really outrageous, beautiful song. This guy was just so good. Years later I wrote Ambulance Blues... and I picked up the melody from his record – the guitar part, exactly – without realizing that I had completely copped the whole thing.'

The album in question was Bert Jansch, recorded for £100 on borrowed guitars in a kitchen. Needle Of Death was a standout favourite and may also have nudged Neil's mind when he wrote The Needle And The Damage Done, given that both songs are about heroin abuse. Jansch's instrumental Angie was another favourite with 1960s crowds and a tune that everyone had to master before anyone would take them seriously as a guitarist. Eric Clapton's sculptured guitar solo on Crossroads was later to have the same effect on amp-using rockers.

I saw Jansch in 1966 at Hull University Union and he had a cunning sense of humour to go along with his delicate, folk-blues picking style. 'Here is a song by Ewan McColl called The First Time Ever I Did See Your Face. And the first time I saw his face I nearly fainted.' Jansch, who went on to some early 1970s glamour, as a founder member of Pentangle, wasn't given similar credit by Led Zeppelin for his Black Water Side which clearly 'inspired' their later Black Mountain Side, although the debate still rages just as Jansch still plays. Young even gives him a credit on Buffalo Springfield Again.

Young did meet Jansch once in England in the early 1970s and got together with Pentangle, whose other members were vocalist Jacqui McShee, John Renbourn, Terry Cox and great bassist Danny Thompson. Apparently they didn't hit it off: 'I had a big limo and everything, because I didn't know where I was going, and they kind of had an attitude about me, like I was a pop superstar and kind of a dickhead.' NY

"Indian

COME ON BABY LET'S GO DOWN TOWN

written by: Danny Whitten/Neil Young
First released: Tonight's The Night (Reprise) **June 1975**

This dazzlingly uncharacteristic live rocker from Tonight's The Night is very much a case of Banquo at the feast. As perhaps the ultimate and most poignant tribute to dead guitarist Danny Whitten, Young included this rousing gem with co-author Whitten taking lead vocals in a performance from the Fillmore East in 1970. Though it hasn't survived in the Young repertoire, the song is an early and infectious example of Neil's rapturous live playing and the high-register backing vocals he was doing with Crosby, Stills And Nash. Perhaps a surprise choice in this collection but in its reminder of what was really lost after Whitten's death, Come On Baby is possibly more effective than anything his band boss could have specially written himself.

This is rock at its best: generous, infective and strangely reminiscent of an unreleased gem from his early solo period, Dance Dance Dance and his much later imploration on Mirror Ball, Downtown. It's also tightly structured around both the chorus and the retrospectively chilling lyric: *'Pretty bad when you're dealing with the Man and the light shines in your eyes,'* which is repeated four times at the song's climax. The first line in this couplet makes the subject clear: *'Sure 'nuff they'll be selling stuff when the moon begins to rise.'* No song of this period so demonstrates the power of music to play across the line of the text: the music and Whitten and Young's guitars defy classification, the two guitar breaks managing to evoke the jagged rock style of Keith Richard but also carrying a hoedown, country feel alongside. This is a song about excitement, going out and boogieing, but it's also a song about drugs, self-delusion and self-destruction. A self-destruction that was, in Whitten's case, only two, no doubt very long, years away.

If you don't tap your feet to this, you're already dead. NY

TONIGHT'S THE NIGHT

First released: Tonight's The Night (Reprise) **June 1975**

The album Tonight's The Night is about ghosts on the road, a recording that came out two years after the nine tracks that form its core were recorded in two sessions at Studio Rentals in Los Angeles. It's an album that remains one of Neil's most revered, a jagged, raw, personal, sometimes vocally incoherent recording fuelled by tequila, beer and countless numbers of joints during long sessions at Neil's home in Topanga. The ghosts in question were Crazy Horse guitarist Danny Whitten and CSN&Y roadie Bruce Berry, whose death, like Whitten's, from a heroin overdose 'out on the mainline', gives this title track its haunting, disturbing opening burst.

It's hard to underestimate the effect of these deaths on Young: both were men he loved, Whitten's death conjuring up the strange absurdity of Eric Dolphy's death much earlier: the visionary alto player going into a diabetic coma at a German airport and, as a black jazz musician, being instantly diagnosed as an OD case and dying through mistreatment. There was nothing to misdiagnose about Whitten though; he was a dyed-in-the-wool junkie by the time Young pulled him in towards the end of 1972 to beef up the guitars on what would have been Neil's first British tour for two years, already scheduled for May the next year with the core of the band already formed from Harvest's The Stray Gators. By this time, Whitten was in such bad shape that Nils Lofgren had to put on his headphones for him and tune his guitar. On 18 November 1972, Whitten finally hit the hot shot, a dose that was almost certainly bought from the $50 Neil had given him to get back to LA. Young had gently thrown him out of rehearsals for being 'too far gone', as Neil told *Rolling Stone*'s Cameron Crowe, innocently conjuring up a term that was to become one of his funniest songs about behavioural and emotional incontinence, featured on the 1989 Freedom album.

Tonight's The Night, the album and the song, are what drummer Ralph Molina later described as an 'Irish wake', a recording imbued by a feeling of collective loss and the desire to push one's feelings as close to the edge as possible. Along with Molina and Billy Talbot from Crazy Horse, the ever-dependable Ben Keith and guitar from the perky, popular Nils Lofgren, Young got so wasted that he later admitted that heroin was not that far from the equation in this attempt to send the boys off into the ether. Right after these sessions, his mind still a mess, Young embarked on his most controversial tour, first of the US, then of the UK, a tour that is now remembered as perhaps his greatest. At the time, it was full of people walking out: those of us who expected tuneful reruns of Harvest were shocked by Young's wasted, gaunt appearance, his lank, unkempt hair, the almost Samuel Beckett touch of turning on a 60-watt bulb to illuminate a single, ludicrous palm tree: 'Welcome to Miami Beach, ladies and gentlemen.' At London's Rainbow, on Guy Fawkes Night, 1973, the fireworks were simply lost on me as Young and the band, temporarily rechristened The Santa Monica Flyers, junked their rock-folk repertoire for new songs from these tragi-comic sessions; Mellow My Mind, World On A String, Albuquerque, the New Mexican town where Neil had his big crack-up on the 1965 road trip from Canada to LA, the retrospectively wonderful and boozy Roll Another Number, the obviously topical Flying On The Ground is Wrong from his Buffalo Springfield days and two insistent,

seemingly endless reruns of Tonight's The Night on a solo piano. 'You can't come back in,' said the man on the door as I left. 'That's OK, I don't want to,' I muttered into the dank, foggy, smoky Finsbury Park night. And hey, shit, I didn't even stick around to hear Cowgirl In the Sand, the concert closer and at least a reminder of supposedly better days. In fact, my most vivid memory was of the support band, tight, musically vibrant and rapturously received. They were called The Eagles and I rushed out and bought what is still their finest album, Desperado.

OK, so I was a schmuck. There were an awful lot of us: the late John Bauldie wrote a marvellous, total-recall piece about the Palace Theatre, Manchester, gig on the same tour for *Mojo*'s special Neil Young supplement in September 1994. The atmosphere sounds similarly raucous and intimidating as the famous Dylan and The Band tour of 1966. Instead of 'Judas!', Young had to contend with appeals to play something 'good', 'Irish', or by the highly-rated Lofgren. Instead of coming back with 'You're a liar,' Young told the hecklers: 'If you can get back to where you were two years ago, I'll get to where I was...'

To almost all of the audience who had no idea about the sessions which led up to this tour, it was a reply as magnificent as it was prophetic, the simple signing-off from a man who's always been one step ahead of the game and has always accepted that music is itself a world on a string. In December 1995's *Mojo*, Young recalled to Nick Kent: 'Oh, that was a fabulous tour, one of my best. Over in England. The Rainbow, Bristol, was the best ever ... the Festival Hall ... those were magical gigs. I did an encore of the latter with nobody there but Ahmet Ertegun, who owns Atlantic records. I said: 'Ahmet, I played so good tonight I think I deserve my own private encore.' So we went out and played Tonight's The Night for the fourth time that evening with no one left in the theatre.'

The album itself wasn't released for some time: the record company uncertain, another more mellow project, Homegrown, pencilled in instead. Only after another boozy playback session at Band member Rick Danko's house did Young's peers insist that he go for this instead. Nobody has put its impact more simply and aptly than Johnny Rogan, who writes in *The Complete Guide To The Music Of Neil Young*: 'Along with On The Beach, this album represented a key moment in 1970s rock, perfectly bridging the gap between singer-songwriter angst and the dawn of punk.'

Indeed, as a recording it conjures up the nightmare world of Charlie Parker's infamous version of Lover Man, recorded after the saxophonist had downed two quarts of whisky and before he returned to set fire to his hotel room. While Parker sounds as if he wants to climb inside his horn and die, grunting, bleating, snuffling and dribbling notes, so Young's voice sounds like it's been roasted over thousands of cigarettes and crates of hard liquor. Never exactly tuneful, Young's voice is always cracking, always out of breath and time. But the record goes a long way to explaining his standing with large numbers of today's MTV-educated Generation X. As Dave Marsh wrote in *Rolling Stone*: 'Crying over the death of his real and imagined friends, Neil Young seems at once heroic and mock heroic, brave and absurd. He leaves us as he found us, ravaged but rocking.' NY

CORTEZ THE KILLER

First released: Zuma (Reprise) **November 1975**

Zuma appeared within four months of Tonight's The Night and Johnny Rogan makes the point that the critical reaction, which was highly enthusiastic, may have been linked to the album's combination of hard-edged rock with a more palatable, commercial, toned-down feel, producing perhaps almost a sense of relief. It was also a great display of the relationship between Young and Crazy Horse, notably with the arrival of Frank 'Poncho' Sampedro to replace the deceased Whitten on rhythm guitar. Billy Talbot had met him in Mexico and at the time, Sampedro told director Jim Jarmusch, he was 'doing heroin and dope' but was also a keen Young fan who had listened to Everybody Knows This Is Nowhere so many times that he could play both Whitten and Young's guitar parts. 'I guess that having a job helped me... in a way we lost one guy and saved another guy.' Sampedro, says Young, brings enormous energy and strength to the band. Certainly, he's an awesomely-built, formidable dude who over the last twenty years has learnt to follow Young's own energy source and float upon it: 'It's always best when I just open up my mind and follow him.'

Zuma wasn't a commercial success, reaching no higher than 44 in the UK album charts, but its reputation has grown, not just because Lou Reed thought the guitar playing on Danger Bird the best he'd ever heard, but because of Cortez The Killer, which remains one of Young's finest accomplishments, not only as a performer but as a more formal, verse-bound lyricist. The song, which comes in at seven and a half minutes, begins slowly and broodingly, a four minute guitar solo which mounts steadily in anticipation and has Young caressing the strings in a thoughtful, patient manner, weaving in and out of Sampedro's accompaniment. It's a good example of why Young prefers the immediacy of live recording to the gadgetry and coldness of overdub. Sampedro's guitar is as a musical equivalent to the second opinion.

When the song starts it is with the deceptively playful and softly sung image of the explorer Cortez *'dancing across the water/with his galleons and guns'*. Only finally does Young echo the sentiments of the title, that this is Cortez The Killer, invader and plunderer of the ancient Aztec civilisation, which is described in tones that are so obviously idealized that the intentions of the song are clear. This is where memory becomes history and finally transmutes itself into myth. The lost civilization of the Aztecs, with its golden temples (gold yet again is Young's imagistic obsession), is a utopia, an empty blackboard on which we can scrawl our own ideas of what life should be like, a life where the individual and the collective become harmonized, a world of angry gods placated by '*clothes of many colours*' and where what was in reality a brutal system of mass human sacrifice which involved cutting out the hearts of living creatures is a formula for regeneration: *'They offered life in sacrifice/so that others could go on.'*

One is reminded of John Ford's classic Western, *The Man Who Shot Liberty Valance*, where a newspaper man advises that where truth and legend diverge it is always wiser to 'print the legend'. Ford's film has one villain and two heroes, the desperado Liberty Valance, played by Lee Marvin, and John Wayne's old-style lawman, the man who finally kills Valance

but allows James Stewart's new-style politician and civilizer to take the credit. Wayne is a glorious frontier anachronism, Stewart's peaceful, quiet-spoken Easterner as much of the future as the railroad which clatters through the whole movie. Young is not interested in history or its 'truth' but in legend, in how we love to view the past from the perspective of our own disquiet with the present. And he makes a final, triumphant point of this when the song shifts finally from ancient Mexico to present day romantic frustration: *'And I know she's living there/And she loves me to this day/I still can't remember when/Or how I lost my way.'* It's a woman, of course, any woman, his, yours or mine, always there like Botticelli's Venus rising from her shell, always lost inside that splendid harmonized world that never existed except in our unfulfilled dreams.

Students so often confuse Cortez and the Aztecs of Mexico with Pizarro and the more pacific Incas of Peru (Neil would also record the linked if less effective Like An Inca for Trans in 1982) that it's worth recalling Peter Shaffer's *The Royal Hunt Of The Sun*, a play with all the light and colours described in this song. It was first seen at the National Theatre in 1964, went to New York in 1965 and covers many of the same themes admittedly only hinted at in the text of Cortez The Killer and Like An Inca: the hypocrisy of martial religion, the nature of power and worship and the necessity to create a society in which a sense of otherworldliness is part of everyday life.

Shaffer also sees the dangers of idealizing ancient civilizations for their own sake: at one point, De Nizza, a subtle Franciscan friar, explains why love is dependent on freedom of choice to the Incas' benevolent despot, Atahualpa: 'Love is the only door from the prison of ourselves.' The final stage direction, after Atahualpa is finally sacrificed to the pragmatism of Spanish conquest and gold worship, and the Western 'god' Pizarro sings over the corpse of the slain Atahualpa, is: 'The sun glares at the audience.' Fanciful or not, there is something despondent and defeated about Young's final guitar flourish; and the surprisingly quick fade-out can seem almost like a hurried apology. NY

LIKE A HURRICANE

First released: American Stars And Bars (Reprise) **September 1976**

Neil Young's most celebrated rocker found its way on to one of his least significant albums, a recording that was to contain a side of American history and a side of bar culture but which ran out of steam in Young's own words because, 'I was drunk on my ass in bars at the time.' He had intended to work on what became Chrome Dreams, a prime staple of the Neil Young bootleg history, but instead wanted a more immediate kind of album. He called Linda Ronstadt in search of a female vocalist and she not only suggested Nicolette Larson but said she'd also come along to Young's ranch. He instantly dubbed them The Saddle Bags and kidded them that they were rehearsing when in fact he was recording, although on their most powerful backing contribution, Bite The Bullet, the two are known as The Bullets. After the debacle of the 1976 tour with Steven Stills and the so-so resultant album, Long May You Run, the title track apart, American Stars And Bars is remarkable only for the inclusion of the amazing Like A Hurricane, which no doubt contributed to its chart showing in the UK of number 12. The song was apparently written as a fond farewell to Carrie Snodgress, with whom he'd lived between 1972 and 1975 and with whom he had son Zeke, whose affliction with cerebral palsy and subsequent learning difficulties were to open a whole new and ultimately inspiring chapter in Neil's life as a man and as a father.

Like A Hurricane remains one of the most celebrated songs in Youngology, not because the image of him soloing away in the face of a gigantic fan is one of the most memorable in rock history but because it's a song about which he's talked at length. In his 1979 interview with Mary Turner to promote the *Rust Never Sleeps* film, Young said: 'If you listen to that, I never actually play anything fast. It's just four notes and the bass keeps going down. Billy plays a few extra notes. The drum beat's the same. It's just a trance we get into, everything starts swimming in circles, and everything starts elevating and it transcends the point of playing fast and slow.'

Neil also talked of the 'soulful feeling' of Crazy Horse, their ability to make him do the most with his music. It's certainly true that nobody plays slo-mo rock better than Young, whose solos on this number have always demonstrated that guitar players with the largest vocabulary often have very little to say. As can be demonstrated from jazz pianist Thelonious Monk's ability to strip bare a song, to dismantle it and find the spaces between the chord changes, a guitar solo is as memorable for its restraint and its inner logic as it is for the kind of crazed pyrotechnics so classically illustrated by Alvin Lee's famous 'show-stopping performance' at Woodstock on I'm Goin' Home. At the time, along with Hendrix's rendition of Star-Spangled Banner, this Ten Years After closer (and it seemed ten years after it finished) was considered the sweat-drenched highlight of the entire movie, now it just seems vulgar and nasty. And thoughtless.

In Like A Hurricane, certainly nowadays on tour when Young can call upon his full armoury of amps, Bigsbys and reverb units, the soloing more than ever takes each chorus into a different musical area, be it through control of volume, use of echo or feedback or a different style of playing. Critics have been ridiculed in the past for daring to find images in this kind of playing (only Jimi Hendrix's Machine Gun bears such a listening approach), but it is impossible not to feel physically changed by this extraordinarily pure and emotionally clear musical expression whether in foot, groin or tensed neck muscle.

This song was featured on the 1976 world tour but by the time of the Rust Never Sleeps concerts Young had built his first 'whizzer', a device that physically turns the knobs on his amplifiers, a four-input '59 Fender Deluxe. According to Larry Cragg, who began working on Neil's guitars in 1971, Young came up with the idea himself: 'Sal Trentino, his amp tech, made the first one. This was a two-position whizzer first used on Rust Never Sleeps in 1978.'

Anyone who's been to a Young concert will notice how he gently activates the pre-arranged settings by pushing footswitches on the red box that's always in front of him, particularly when he changes to a pickup technique on his black Les Paul. In December 1991, Young did tell *Musician* magazine: 'I have no technique! I do have technique but you don't really recognize it as anything but noise.' Ain't it easy to be humble, given that the volume controls go from a presumably hushed six to the legendary, eardrum-blasting eleven?

Actually, though Young can be staggeringly inept these days in talking about his guitar style ('It sucks,' etc.), he reserves most of his best interview performances for the specialist guitar magazines. In the March 1992 issue of *Guitar Player*, Jas Obrecht asked Young about his earlier remark that jamming was like having an orgasm (something Paul Gascoigne has said about scoring a goal): 'Well, yeah,' replied Young. 'That's why a lot of my instrumentals are too short!' Funny, Neil, but tell that to the people who've listened to the whole of Arc/Weld.

In fact, when it comes to musicians who won't play ball, Mick Jagger is still the champion. I once asked Mick what his favourite Stones album was. 'What's yours?' he replied. 'Let it Bleed.' 'Oh yeah... What's on it?'

There is a wonderful coda to the history of this song at the climax of Jim Jarmusch's documentary film *Year Of The Horse*. Poncho Sampedro, the butchest, most plain-speaking member of Crazy Horse, launches into a good-natured attack on Jarmusch who he wrongly describes as a 'hip, trendy, artsy-fartsy New York producer.' Jarmusch corrects him: he is, a fter all, a writer-director. 'This film,' opines Poncho, 'doesn't even scratch the tip of the iceberg. This band has been so many changes, in lifestyles, families, venues and the ways we record and the instruments we used and loving each other and hating each other and the whole deal.' The film cuts to Like A Hurricane, first to a Roman ampitheatre on the banks of the Rhône in 1996, with Young matted and middle-aged, playing out of his skin; then it cuts instantly and stunningly back twenty years in time without hardly a break in the voice, to the Hammersmith Odeon gig of March 1976. Young was even using the same guitar. The film returns to 1996, this time to a gig at the Gorge in Washington State, and a frenzied free-form, sheet-of-sound finale which has drummer Ralph Molina soloing into space, Poncho chaking his instrument, Young deconstructing his 1952 Old Black Les Paul, pounding its strings as it lies on the floor. Lights flash and whirr, arpeggios and feedback of pure white noise drench the audience. A proof that time is not all-conquering and a fine end to an exemplary rock documentary. NY

HUMAN HIGHWAY

First released: Comes A Time (Reprise) **September 1978**

Following on from the triple album retrospective, Decade, in 1977, Comes A Time is quite simply Neil Young's best non-rock recording. His voice, which even the sceptical Dave Marsh has compared with that of the great Delta bluesman Skip James, has never sounded richer or more confident. The playing and the recording balance is sublime and Young is clearly careful to avoid the pitfalls of over-elaboration from the Harvest days. The songs are so good that it's hard to know which to choose from the skidding strings-and-fiddles jauntiness of the title track (*'Lift that baby right up off the ground'*), the acoustic dramas of Look Out For My Love and Peace Of Mind, the touching maturity of Already One (like the later Separate Ways, a hymn to the unshatterable bonds of parenthood) or the countrified optimism of Field Of Opportunity. Even Lotta Love, which Young released as a 12-inch disco single in 1982, proved to be a top ten hit for the woman whose voice permeated this recording with supportive charm (Motorcycle Mama apart, that is): Nicolette Larson. Sadly, Larson was to die tragically young from a brain-fluiddisorder on 16 December 1997, aged forty five.

It's also proof that Young's often pernickety approach to sound quality can bring the best results: Comes A Time is an album with a very long credits list, not just Crazy Horse plus saxophonist and co-producer Tim Mulligan, but the amusingly titled Gone With The Wind orchestra, whose line-up included the haunting steel guitar of Young dependable Ben Keith, the awesome Spooner Oldham on piano, Steve Gibson on acoustic, and even JJ Cale providing the occasional lick on electric guitar. It was recorded at a variety of locations; Young's ranch in Redwood City, Fort Lauderdale, Columbia Studios in London, and (mostly) Nashville.

Human Highway is the most perplexed and despondent song on Comes A Time, a quiet hymn-like meditation on the unkindness of strangers with the grim, repeated imploration, *'Take my eyes from what they've seen.'* Young revived it for his last live album, 1996's Year Of The Horse, where it sounds even more contemplative despite all the beefed-up electricity. This was a happy time for Neil: 'I was feeling pretty sunny,' he told *Rolling Stone*'s Cameron Crowe at the time, having taken his son Zeke on a 'cross-country ride on his tour bus' and got well into one of his favourite hobbies, the collection of antique cars. The writer and film-maker Ernie Eban knew Young around this time and recalls how, sometime in 1976, Young had been persuaded to part-fund a project aimed at teaching a gorilla called Koko sign language and had even taken a course himself: 'It was later taken up by the National Geographic.' Crowe also hints at a brief romantic liaison with Larson, whose duet with Young on Already One was a musical tribute to his past relationship with Carrie Snodgress and the son who 'won't let us forget'.

Johnny Rogan, in *The Complete Guide To The Music Of Neil Young*, notes that this song was originally considered for the title track of Crosby, Stills, Nash And Young's 'lost second album' and was also a favourite in concert, where Young would sometimes play around with the lyrics. Indeed, the song was laid down originally during sessions that the Stills/Young Band did at Criteria Studios in Miami in April 1976. The duo were joined by David Crosby and Graham Nash to work on a bunch of songs, almost ready for release, but when the two left to complete their new album, Whistle Down the Wire, Stills and Young showed their Machiavellian streak by

wiping Nash and Crosby's vocal contributions off the tracks, Human Highway included. Nash, quoted in *Neil Young: The Visual Documentary*: 'I must admit I was surprised to hear from Neil. But I was intrigued by this project he was doing with Stephen. When he came by my house and played me and David a tape of the things they'd done– Black Coral, Midnight On The Bay, Human Highway – they sounded great. Then Neil said: "Isn't there somethin' missing?" Crosby goes: "Yeah, us." So the next morning we were on the plane to Miami.' Stills asserted that it was 'Neil's idea to take David and Graham's vocals off our tracks'. Nash: 'Fuck 'em. I will not work with them again.'

Human Highway was also the title of the never-released movie which Young started in May 1978 with Dean Stockwell, his friend from After The Goldrush days who was pencilled in as director and co-writer. The film, to be shot on Young's ranch in Taos, New Mexico, also involved talents as varied as Devo and Dennis Hopper, but its fate was to be somewhat gazumped by the Rust Never Sleeps tour and movie.

At the time of the album's release, Young was beginning to feel the effect of the British new wave. In 1978, people were turned on to bands like The Sex Pistols, The Police, The Specials, Squeeze, Graham Parker And The Rumour and Elvis Costello And The Attractions. But this became his best-selling album since Harvest in the UK, where it reached number seven in the charts as against a rather dismal number 42 in America. NY

FOUR STRONG WINDS

Written by: Ian Tyson

First released: Comes A Time (Reprise) **September 1978**

Critics seem divided on this album closer, which gave Young a minor UK single hit when it crashed into the Top 60 at number 57. Unlike every other song on this list, it wasn't written by Young but is a cover of what the unimpressed Johnny Rogan calls 'Ian Tyson's folk chestnut'. It's intriguing that Young chose this song with its direct call to his Winnipeg folk roots and Canadian youth: written in 1963 and released a year later, it was a massive hit for Tyson and his partner, later wife, Sylvia Fricker, who, as Ian And Sylvia, were one of the most successful folk acts to emerge from Toronto. The duo performed at the Mariposa Folk Festival for the first time in 1961 and by the time this, their second single, had been released they had toured around the folk clubs of New York and Chicago.

David Downing believes that Young's voice has never been more 'seductively plaintive', while Greil Marcus, reviewing the album in *Rolling Stone*, gave it special attention: 'When Young closes out his story with Ian Tyson's Four Strong Winds, there's a real sense of time having passed, of choices made and chances blown. The wistfulness of Tyson's song doesn't survive Young's refusal to cater to its prettiness.' Marcus found himself thinking of Bob Dylan's If You See Her, Say Hello and Shelter From The Storm. Undoubtedly, Young's arrangement is both majestic and controlled, the chiming swoops of the guitar perfectly attuned to Ben Keith's weeping pedal steel and Nicolette Larson's charming, underpinning vocal. Brilliantly, Marcus notes that what originally seemed a tune of internalized whimsy becomes dramatic, as if Neil was talking 'plain talk' to 'a real person'. I can't improve on that, but even Marcus couldn't know that this astonishing piece of folk fatalism was to be placed in Young's canon between the hard-rockings of American Stars And Bars and Rust Never Sleeps.

Folk music has always been given a rough ride by certain members of the rock critic fraternity who like to dismiss it as holding-hands, real-ale music for the knitted muesli brigade. Odd that my own first experiences of folk came from listening to Martin Carthy and Dave Swarbrick, whose stunning debut album opened with High Germany, a traditional song about the wife of a man pressed into service and forced to fight for his Hanoverian king in European wars. The woman bewails her fate: maybe she was the same one who perished on the gallows for stealing cloth to cover her child, an incident used by Charles Dickens in the introduction to *Barnaby Rudge*. To dismiss all folk music as nostalgic, prettified tosh is like calling the Old Romantics a bunch of drug-sodden, frilly-shirt wearing posers: Keats was a surgeon; Wordsworth rode and walked countless miles and travelled to revolutionary France; Byron fought in the ring and for the liberation of Greece.

Four Strong Winds is a small masterpiece, in which Young really does remind us about the chains that bind and the forces that pull. If I ever die, I want it played at my funeral. NY

LYNYRD SKYNYRD'S
OLD TIME
Old

POWDERFINGER

First released: Rust Never Sleeps (Reprise) **June 1979**

Indubitably one of Neil's finest ever songs, a bracing live belter, a wistful anthem to doomed youth, notably in Young's own unreleased Chrome Dreams twelve-string acoustic version (you can understand every word!) and in the sombre, elegiac cover by the wonderful Cowboy Junkies. It's also one of Neil's best songs about American history, a sign of what the history side of American Stars And Bars might have been like if Neil hadn't dumped most of the project.

Young once admitted that he couldn't write 'more than half a page at a time' and couldn't get on with reading scripts. Yet this would make a fantastic opener (or closer) to a film by Howard Hawks or Sam Peckinpah. *'Look out, mama, there's a white boat comin' up the river'*, ushers in this poignant tale of one young man's reluctant heroism on a clearly domestic note. This is a civil war, a civilian war, men don't go to combat with their mothers in tow, not even when they're merely *'22 and wonderin' what to do'*. Men in foreign wars don't worry about calling John *'because I don't think they're here/To deliver the mail'*. Or get lumbered with hopeless odds because *'the powers that be have left me here to do the thinking'*.

Powderfinger could be tied to the American War Of Independence, but several fans have wondered whether the setting isn't more contemporary and the aggressive boat in question isn't simply 'a coastguard cutter' looking for illegal stills activity. After all, Big John has *'been drinking since the river took Emmylou'*. Powderfinger is a song that most obviously compares with the best output of his Canadian brothers The Band, an outfit who at their considerable best rescued music from love-torn mediocrity and introduced a sweep and a sense of the past that conjured up the worlds of Mark Twain, Stephen Crane, John Steinbeck and William Faulkner. For Powderfinger, with its Old Mississippi-style setting, is Young's least preachy statement on the American South, a far more objective take than Southern Man or Alabama.

The Band made the template for this with The Night They Drove Old Dixie Down, a mournful song inspired, says Robbie Robertson, by a trip to Levon Helm's father's house during which Helm Senior said in a thick Southern voice tinged with irony: 'You know, one day, Robbie, the South will rise again.' The Band's masterpiece was a deeply unfashionable song at the time, one that saw the Civil War not in terms of easy moral arguments but as a great human tragedy from which large parts of America have never fully emerged. (Rather similar to Steve Earle's superbly angry Ben McCullough, written back home in Tennessee, Earle once told me, when he was a mere lad of 14.)

The linking verse remains as fine an example of Civil War poetry as any ever penned. Virgil Cain's brother is four years younger than the doomed hero of Powderfinger, one year younger than the average age of the combatants in the Vietnam conflict, famously known from pop history to be 19.

One of the most searing images from the Vietnam war were the field hospitals, from which daily news bulletins beamed home pictures of mortally-wounded young men panting, moaning and screaming out their last on blood-stained operating tables. Like the man in the song, who raises his rifle to his eye, never stops to wonder why, sees black and his face splash in the sky, these were young men, boys, who had *to 'fade away so young/With so much left undone'.* Men who never had the chance to live and didn't even have the chance to die in their own backyard.

The last verse is awesome, asking (in less inspired words), spare me the violence of people who have both the means and the opportunity; cover me, bury me, hide me, from the black hatred that caused my demise. In concert, Young often reserves his finest solos for this song. Never over-elaborated and flashy, his guitar work literally sobs, rising and falling, moving subtly from major to minor chords in the process, really focusing the instrumental on the song's massive sense of human loss.

There is one particularly fine example of this on a bootleg recording of Young's 1993 tour with Booker T And The MGs in the Belgian city of Ghent. How They Brought The Good News From Aix To Ghent goes the famous poem. Neil spent the entire evening moaning about his tuning, the acoustics, the audience ('You're very quiet... Make some noise. Rub your girlfriend or something. We're only here for a short time. You might as well get it while you can.'). Obviously the 'good news' hadn't reached him, but Powderfinger was a blast.

On the Internet, the song has given rise to a wonderful lengthy debate: 'Look out, mama, There's a big discussion comin' up.' Such questions raised include: Did the young man shoot himself or was he killed? Did the rifle backfire? Is the man on the dock an Indian, hence the arrival of a 'white boat'? Is 'Daddy' the absent brains behind a drugs operation? And isn't it just a song about make-up? NY

POCAHONTAS

First released: Rust Never Sleeps (Reprise) **June 1979**

M*arlon Brando, Pocahontas and me.'* These could well be the five most charming words Young's ever written, in which – like the song – he links himself with history both ancient and modern. Young wrote Pocahontas after seeing Sasheen Littlefeather, the native American rights activist, take Marlon Brando's 1972 Best Actor Oscar for *The Godfather*. Above all else, Pocahontas is a delightful piece of songwriting with a jaunty, country guitar feel and lyrics that are simultaneously funny, anecdotal, detached and angry.

The rights of native Americans and the dignity of lost ancient cultures are recurring themes in Young's music, from Broken Arrow to Cortez The Killer *(see earlier entries)*.

While Pocahontas is named after the sixteenth century princess who saved the life of English explorer John Smith and was later to feature in a ludicrous piece of Disney cartoon anti-Englishness, the song's images of persecution come from four centuries on. *'They massacred the buffalo, and they cut our women down/They might have left some babies lying on the ground.'* The images were fashionable in that period in the late 1960s and early 1970s, when the rights of people who, it seemed, were almost perceived as a kind of superior type of hippy were so eagerly expounded. In 1970, two years before Brando's Oscar, came Ralph Nelson's highly successful anti-racist film, *Soldier Blue*, in which the massacre at Sand Creek in 1864 was seen from the point of view of Candice Bergen's confused eyewitness and the Sioux who were murdered, raped and butchered there.

Young's take on the native American could be slandered as cosy, the kind of safe, at-arms-length issue so popular with non-politicals who like to see themselves as more than dollar-seeking celebrities. Similar accusations were levelled against Christopher Hampton's play about the destruction of the Brazilian Indians, *Savages*, premiered in London in 1973 and seen in Young's neighbouring Los Angeles a year later. Young brings his own youthful interest in these things to the forefront of the song via a verse dealing with *'his little box at the top of the stairs/with an Indian rug and a pipe to share'.*

But just as this is a case of childhood role-playing, so Pocahontas is an elegy for a past civilization that we mourn without the gift of understanding, real memory or any real alternative. They may have '*the Astrodome and the first tepee*' on show in Hollywood now, but does that really make us long for a return to the wilderness years when the buffalo roamed? Are the 'redskins' only lovable simply because they've now been obliterated by assimilation?

There's a wonderful take on the complexity of this in George MacDonald Fraser's *Flashman And The Redskins* (1982), in which Fraser's immortally scoundrellish Flashman relives two periods of his life: in the 1840s among the scalp hunters and Apaches of New Mexico, and in the 1870s with the Sioux, the classic noble savages of popular imagination. Flashman even becomes big buddies with the native American cavalry leader after whom Young's best band is named, Crazy Horse. The book begins with an octogenarian Flashman involved in a verbal ruckus with a gentleman's-club liberal who despairs of the way the noble Indian has been let down by Washington and roundly condemns the barbarities of Custer and Skivvington.

General Flashman, irritated, tired and emotional, enters the conversation by showing his scalp wound received from a Brule knife at the Battle Of The Little Big Horn: *'And you burble about enlightenment, by God – try to enlighten a Comanche war party, why don't you? Suggest humanity and restraint to the Jicarillas who carved up Mrs White and her baby on Rock Creek! Have you ever seen a Del Norte rancho after the Mimbreno have left their calling cards? No, not you, you plush-bottomed bastard ... I've a damned sight more use for the Indian than you have ... as much as I have for the rest of humanity, at all events ... and I don't make 'em an excuse for parading my own virtue while not caring a fig for them, as you do, so there!'*

Well, it's a point of view. NY

MY MY, HEY HEY (OUT OF THE BLUE)

First released: Rust Never Sleeps (Reprise) **June 1979**

This song, which Young often uses as a rousing let's-start-the-show-right-here opener, is now a very sad metaphor for his credentials in the 1990s; so ironic that a piece which celebrates the survival of rock 'n' roll is now so inextricably linked with the suicide, on 5 April 1993, of Nirvana's Kurt Cobain, that Young publicly declared his intention of abandoning it from his public performances. Recently, he has rightly gone back on this decision. Artists can do that, of course: Stanley Kubrick withdrew *A Clockwork Orange* from British outlets after it became tenuously connected with a violent death; Lou Reed once intoned 'I'm gonna do Heroin for the guys at the front,' but has now ditched that dose of white heat for more political statements on drugs and New York; even Elton John has blown out his Candle In The Wind after the Princess Diana rewrite.

Maybe this decision, taken after news that Cobain had quoted Young's line that 'it's better to burn out than to fade away', has almost irritated Young's fans, one of whom took the trouble to write to *Broken Arrow* fanzine about Cobain's failure to understand the positive nature of a song which salutes Elvis Presley and Johnny Rotten in almost the same breath. Cobain undoubtedly had his own set of problems at the time of his death and could just as easily have scrawled in red ink: 'To be or not to be, that is the question.'

Then again, Cobain isn't the only deceased rock superstar to take umbrage with the sentiments apparent from this line. David Shelf, in a *Playboy* interview with John Lennon in September 1980, only two months before Lennon's death, asked the Beatle what he thought of the line and Lennon pitched in: 'I hate it. It's better to fade away like an old soldier than to burn out. If he was talking about burning out like Sid Vicious, forget it. I don't appreciate the worship of dead Sid Vicious or of dead James Dean or dead John Wayne. It's the same thing ... I worship the people who survive ... Gloria Swanson, Greta Garbo.'

Young directly disagreed with Lennon's interpretation two years later: 'Of course the people who play rock 'n' roll should survive. But the essence of rock 'n' roll spirit to me is that it's better to burn out really bright than to sort of decay into infinity.' But that's basically the same thing he told Mary Turner in 1979 in a Warners interview released as a promotional CD: 'People expect stars to be flashy. Stars are supposed to represent something greater, bigger than life. It's better to burn out because it makes a bigger flash.'

It seems we're heading for a philosophical log-jam here: not only a half-hearted attempt to square artistic with bodily survival, but with an extra dose of O-level astronomy attached. Ironically, of course, it's Neil Young who has embodied the third alternative on a career level, by neither burning out nor fading away, but constantly recharging his batteries by his magpie absorption of new fashions and varied musical styles, something he alluded to at the time when he told Turner: 'The longer I keep going, the longer I have to fight this corrosion.' Without a doubt, the live concert from which this version was taken underlines Young's appreciation of his own musical past, underscored with music from Jimi Hendrix and The Beatles.

Though it doesn't appear until sixth on the song list, My My, Hey Hey is a key moment in the *Rust Never Sleeps* movie which Young brought out under the name of Bernard Shakey and

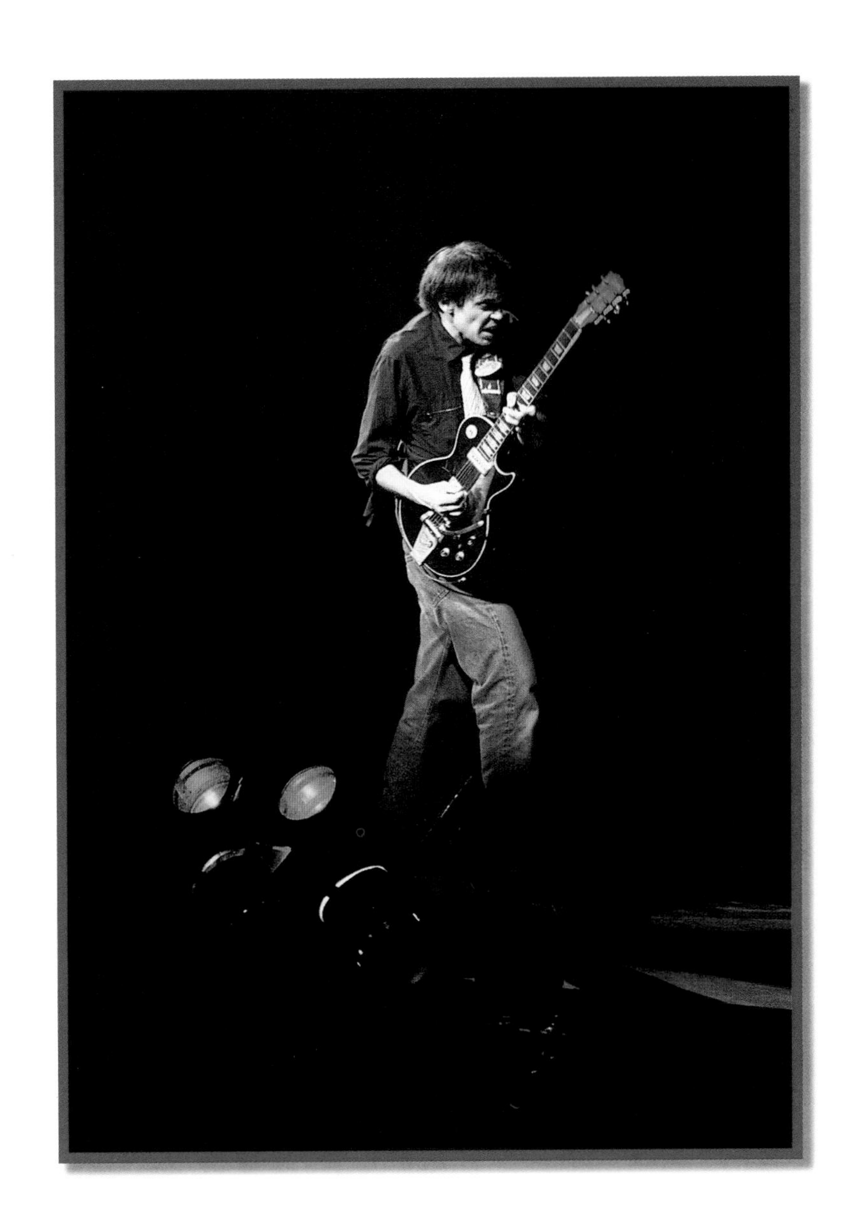

may well have been the prime reason that *Village Voice* voted him Artist Of The Decade; in 1987, *Rolling Stone* called it 'one of the greatest live performances of the last twenty years'.

The tour in question, released in part as the accompanying Live Rust album the same month as the film, and as glimpsed from the video of the film recorded at the Cow Palace, San Francisco, on 22 October 1978, was obviously remarkable musically, but its history and design are more difficult to take seriously after Rob Reiner's classic rock satire, *This Is Spinal Tap*. Rather like most medieval movies ('Men of the Middle Ages, welcome to the Hundred Years War!') are after *Monty Python And The Holy Grail*.

Young gives us the Roadeyes, pint-sized stage-crew members with glowing eyes, hooded like friars, who manhandle equipment, a giant microphone and stand, a massive tuning fork and an outsized baggy sleeping bag which the rather Little Ab'ner-esque Young crawls into at the end of the acoustic set. It's hard not to think of the sequence in which Spinal Tap's attempt to use a model backdrop of Stonehenge is ruined when the measurements are found to be in inches rather than feet.

The Roadeyes certainly caused one of Young's more bizarre brushes with litigation: after the pop music critic of the *Los Angeles Times* had noted a similarity with the Jawas from George Lucas's film, *Star Wars*, Young and his lawyers had to make an out-of-court settlement with the film company Twentieth Century-Fox over use of them on album, film and bill-board advertisements. Doubly amusing given that Young has confessed that he did have a special affection for *Star Wars*, which he thought was 'brilliant'.

My My, Hey Hey is another Young song blessed with an instantly distinctive opening hook and a classic example of his facility for mixing backswing strumming with finger-picking; it's almost like a basic blues has been transformed into an anthem, the chords changing from A Minor through G to A with F as the bass-note. Co-credited to Jeff Blackburn, a former Moby Grape member whom Young had known since his days with The Ducks, the album closes with its coda, Hey Hey, My My (Into The Black) which, as Johnny Rogan has noted, is almost exactly the same song, though performed electrically with Crazy Horse, as My My, Hey Hey.

One key change that does occur is that Young turns the statement 'this is the story of Johnny Rotten' into a question, which could betray ambivalence or just laziness. Young's somewhat casual attitude to lyrics was evinced in the interview he gave to Mary Turner, when he mentioned his collaborations at the time with Ohio's own Devo, who had been doing advertising work for a 'rust inhibitor' and had been using the slogan in their work. NY

CAPTAIN KENNEDY

First released: Hawks And Doves (Reprise) **October 1980**

In one of those remarkable incidents of rock lore, the feedback answer to discovering a new play by Shakespeare, an acetate of the abandoned Chrome Dreams album turned up in the early 1990s, including the whole, re-ordered second side of American Stars And Bars, Look Out For My Love from Comes A Time and this track from Hawks And Doves, Young's largely uninspired opener to his most perplexing and difficult decade.

Captain Kennedy is a fascinating song, a folkie that has a traditional sound but lyrics crafted by Young himself, a song which both broods, Powderfinger-style, about the horrors of war while bracingly conjuring up the pleasures of a seafaring existence. Cleverly, it's also a song that unites these threads by being both patriotic (*'and humiliate that American, Captain Kennedy'*) and dutiful, the story told by a son about his father. As Johnny Rogan notes, the song bears a striking similarity to Steve Stills' Know You've Got To Run, which was combined with Young's Everybody I Love You on the CSN&Y Deja Vu album, although only Young's part was reflected in the title of what ended up as an upbeat finale to the 1970 hit. Captain Kennedy also reminds me strangely of the traditional Scottish poem and song, *The Ballad Of Sir Patrick Spens*, which begins '*The King sits in Dunfermline toon, drinking the blood-red wine/Saying, "Who will find me a seely skipper to sail yon ship of mine?".*'

There are intriguing non-textual minutiae clinging to this song: its obvious love of the sea life could be linked to the work Young did between 1976 and 1978 on the rebuilding of a sailing boat, reminiscent of 'the wooden schooner' that Kennedy lost to the Germans. The craft, the WN Ragland, named after his maternal grandfather, was the boat in which Young sailed on his honeymoon with blonde beauty Pegi Morton.

Morton, one of the great, enduring loves of Young's life, had met him socially in the mid-1970s in the San Mateo County hills, where he had a ranch and where she grew up, but the relationship was rekindled in earnest around Christmas 1977, shortly after the abrupt disintegration of his short romance with Nicolette Larson. Ironically, as the song was written well before Young's courtship and marriage to Pegi, there's the line *'I met him in Nassau in 1971'*, the couple choosing the Bahamas as their honeymoon destination after their marriage on 2 August 1978. What seems certain are the links to Young's father, Scott, who was a wartime seaman in the Canadian navy and even made the rank of sub-lieutenant by the last year of the conflict. The use of the name 'Kennedy' has given rise to speculation that it's also linked to the well-documented wartime heroics of fellow navy man John F Kennedy (Young wrote an adolescent guitar instrumental – who didn't? – in memory of JFK's assassination), but the name has a fine ring to it within the context of the song and pleasing coincidence seems more likely.

Young reached the end of the 1970s immensely successful, established as a staggeringly versatile and individual voice, an enduring talent who was also in love and happily married. But by the time this album appeared, his life had been ravaged, first by the terrible news in 1979 that his and Pegi's son Ben, born in November 1978, was afflicted, like older son Zeke, by cerebral palsy. The odds on this happening to two different children with the same parent are literally a million to one. Like all parents (my own son William was born the same year in June and mercifully healthy), the guilt and anguish must have been massive, especially from a man who has himself endured childhood polio and, later, epilepsy. No wonder there's a dark side to Young: and this wasn't to be the end.

In March 1980, Pegi Young was diagnosed as suffering from a brain tumour, thankfully recovering after an operation in September that year. The couple set off on the boat again, this time for Tahiti, onetime resting place of Fletcher Christian and the other Bounty mutineers. Like Christian, or the painter Paul Gauguin, Young must have mused on the strange tricks of fate. NY

SHOTS

First released: RE-AC-TOR, (Reprise) **October 1981**

Though Shots is the only memorable thing about this last Reprise album before Young moved to Geffen Records in 1982, this section is very much the Essential Steve Grant. The early 1980s were a troubled time for Neil Young and his family, most of whose creative energies were taken up with son Ben's treatment for cerebral palsy, which involved all concerned in the radical, all-embracing therapy of the Programme. Young completed work on *Human Highway* the movie in June 1982 but nobody wanted to release it, damning it as 'too weird'. This album sold badly, wasn't publicized properly and despite a reunion with Crazy Horse and the feedback drenched power of this, its last ,seven-minutes plus track, it lacked energy and point. Young was elsewhere and in 1982 his disorientations were reflected in his open support for the presidency of Ronald Reagan, his dismissal of anti-nuclear festival performers as 1960s nostalgists and his avowal to a French journalist that he was 'a bigger capitalist than most Americans!'

Young's endorsement of Reaganite America, though not quite so damning as Eric Clapton's drunken stage announcement that 'Enoch Powell is right!' a few years earlier, caused disenchantment and disbelief. When a twenty-something colleague heard I was writing this book, she brought it up immediately, as if Neil had joined the KKK or the Nazi Brotherhood. But the early 1980s were a tough time for many of us, coming to terms with Thatcherism in Britain and the right-wing shift across the Atlantic, particularly those of us who saw the certainties of the previous two decades evaporating, saw simple truths becoming at best half-truths.

Personally, this period and notably 1981, was the worst of my life. I had started as a journalist on the communist *Morning Star*, moved to the *Camden Journal*, part of a North London newspaper group and one of the most radical local newspapers in the country, always on strike it seemed and now a collective; and, after a brief stint at the non-union, boldly reactionary *Plays And Players*, had ended up in 1976 at *Time Out*, which I'd fallen in love with after reading an article by Jonathon Green about a restaurant in Islington which served mice on the menu. Years later I found out it was a spoof.

By 1981, *Time Out* was involved in a bitter, 12-week dispute which almost closed down the magazine for good, led to the creation of two, now-defunct rivals, the co-operative *City Limits* and Richard Branson's *Event*, and caused hateful divisions between people who had previously worked together as friends. I once read in a women's magazine that the most stressful things that can happen in life are marital break up, unemployment, serious illness and bereavement. In 1981, I lost my job because of the strike, learned that I was diabetic, started to break up with my wife and, though nobody close to me died, the year was topped off nicely when hated Spurs won the FA Cup. I watched the match in the occupied *Time Out* offices in Covent Garden with two Tottenham fans who happened to be lesbians. When the final whistle went, the butch one planted a sloppy kiss on my mouth. Happy days.

There was a great deal of sneering about the *Time Out* dispute: Ian Jack wrote a contemptuous piece in *The Sunday Times* headlined: 'Gravy Train derailed: few casualties'. Of course, Jack's newspaper was soon to be plunged into its own, much more violent and well-publicized dispute at Wapping, when Rupert Murdoch locked out the print unions and picket line violence was extremely nasty. *Time Out*'s dispute was a microcosm of this, but also one that centred around a concept that oozed both Marxism and hippy togetherness and, amazingly, a concept that I'd experienced twice in my relatively short career: Parity.

Parity meant equal pay for all: in theory terrific, particularly in blue collar factory situations, and absolutely hunky-dory if it begins at birth in a perfect world. At the *Morning Star* it was a complete farce: it applied only to editorial staff. The print workers, members of the National Graphical Association, the gang bosses of Fleet Street, were given the full national newspaper whack, even though their staff at the time comprised only one Communist Party member who'd joined before working there, anyway, many convinced Tory voters and even a smattering of avowed racists.

The journalists, all idealistic and committed, were paid the same, so all were equally skint in theory, although most were Fleet Street and BBC veterans who'd made their pile, champagne Marxists with rich partners or private incomes and people like the Sports Editor, whose one Saturday shift on a Sunday newspaper earned him double his weekly salary from the *Star*. There's a delicious story about the then editor who got a puncture cycling home and was given a lift by a printer driving a Jag. Ah, the contradictions of socialism.

The rest, like me, were young unattached singles who, even in the very early 1970s, found it hard to live on £14 a week. (In the first days of parity, *Daily Worker* – as it was then known – journos actually had to hand money back at the pay desk as part of their 'covenant' to keep the paper's future out of danger from right-wing anti-communist union bosses. At least that misery had gone by the time I arrived.)

When I joined *Time Out*, I didn't even know that parity was the order of the day, but it didn't bother me, I was just happy to be there. Everyone from the switchboard operators to the editor on the same, liveable wage? OK by me, comrade cutie! But by the early 1980s, the divisions had become intolerable. Union disputes were constant, often over trivial matters: one whole issue was lost because of a supposedly sexist and exploitative ad for Brian De Palma's *Dressed To Kill*. It didn't matter that the ad was running all over London, or that the woman in a dress whose knee was visible to the sinister man appearing at the door was, in fact, Michael Caine in drag.

By 1981, fed up with what Janet Street-Porter once dubbed the 'spirit of Toytown', *Time Out*'s management were determined to break the code of parity. Though several of us were now married with children and mortgages, no one on the staff caved in and I still blame both sides, particularly as the management had let things slide before putting their foot down. But the union situation was irritating beyond belief. In my previous jobs, union membership was rigorously enforced and only full-time staffers could attend chapel meetings and vote. At *Time Out*, with its ludicrous air of hippy Trotskyism, the attitude was 'the more the merrier'. When we decided to call the 'big' strike, those of us on one income, family-supporting, five-day-a-week full-timers voted alongside temporary holiday replacements and part-timers, one of

whom had a four-day gig at the *Observer* newspaper and who promptly disappeared for the strike's entirety. Others were writing books or articles for newspapers (me included), some had very rich parents or partners, others just didn't give a fuck beyond posturing in union meetings that had far more to do with anthropology than politics, more Desmond Morris than Arthur Scargill. Our then Music Editor, John Collis, used to joke wonderfully that 'the chapel are sticking out for eternal life'.

I'm not proud of my own behaviour: after twelve weeks of entrenchment, lock-outs and exile at the Drill Hall strike HQ, where they served hideous bright green soup which still gives me the shudders, with the Grants dangerously near to losing our home, I'd had enough. I freelanced for the *Guardian* newspaper, joined Branson's *Event* and eventually returned to *Time Out*, glad that it survived and certain that most of the founder members of *City Limits* would be soon off to well-paid, non-parity jobs elsewhere. Those that could get them, that is.

I'm even less proud of the pompous lies that were told about the dispute by the chattering brigade: how one charming *NME* soul stated bravely that the dispute 'separated the sheep from the goats', which didn't stop her abjectly seeking work with us some time later. Or the parties I went to, where saying you worked for *Time Out* was like admitting a connection with the Kray Twins. Or the meeting of the Magazine Branch of the NUJ where our then news reporter, David Rose, now a senior campaigning journalist, was almost expelled on a trumped-up charge of racism by a committee headed by someone who worked for *Caged Birds* magazine. Calling David Rose a racist is rather like claiming that the Pope is a Presbyterian. Rose, a Jew, has distinguished himself on stories about the ultra-right, the Toxteth and Broadwater Farm riots, the case of Winston Silcott and many other matters. But, of course, he did work for *Time Out*.

Typically, the presence of the gang-bosses of the NGA was again much in evidence, leather-coated swaggerers who blew cigar-smoke in our faces and began each speech with 'Our members will...' – the same people who used to stop newspapers coming out because a desk had been moved a foot to the wrong side, a roll of paper had turned up late or because the management had tried to discipline someone who did three shifts a night around Fleet Street and signed himself 'Donald Duck'. As Tom Stoppard pointed out in his play *Night And Day*, journalists in foreign war zones risked their very lives for stories that didn't appear for the absurdest of reasons.

I was bitter then, but not now. Most of my former political enemies are now my friends and we've all changed. But I'm a creature of contradiction just like Neil Young was in 1982: after Vietnam and Carter's embarrassment over the Iranian hostages, even someone like Reagan must have looked good – regardless of the fact that Ronald Reagan can't order breakfast without cue cards. Similarly, my working class pedigree, for what it's worth, is pretty impeccable: my mum and dad both left school at 14: but while I can forgive Margaret Thatcher little, I don't miss the print unions or the bullshit about 'equal pay' one little bit. NY

SAMPLE AND HOLD

First released: Trans (Geffen) **January 1983**

Dinosaurs in the computer age.' Thus spake Neil Young for his Transband at the end of several concerts on the European tour of 1982, the first live concert journey that Young had undertaken since Rust Never Sleeps four years earlier. The decision to choose Europe could be explained thus: Young's European fans had missed out then and Europe in general, and Germany in particular, where the tour climaxed, was the home of the computerized sound that was to dominate his creativity during this Trans-sitional time.

The musical influence of the visionary Dusseldorf outfit Kraftwerk cannot be underestimated here. The band formed by Ralf Hutter and Florian Schneider and three cohorts in Dusseldorf in 1969 had dented the US album charts in May of 1981 with Computer World, a clear homage to which was to appear on Trans, Young's first album for his new label Geffen, in his song Computer Age. Kraftwerk's status in pop history is substantial: between Autobahn in 1974 and The Mix in 1991, Hutter and Schneider developed a method where music wasn't so much created as constructed. By the late 1990s their influence on modern music encompassed everything from electro and techno to house and ambient, and the output of everyone from Portishead, Orbital, Inner City, Leftfield and Prodigy, to LFO and Underworld.

Kraftwerk's influence is at the musical heart of Trans, which is dominated by five tracks all employing computerized effects and the vocal distortions of the vocoder, a small machine attached to a microphone wire which could feed the human voice into a computer and allow it both the freedom of a four-octave range and the perfection and elongation of machine-made sound. In August 1981, Young bought himself a vocoder and started to record a group of songs that were to eventually appear on Trans, initially in his own upgraded studio, improved to take into account the restrictions in his professional life imposed by his son Ben's learning disabilities. Here, then, we have another and more poignant link to Young's thinking at the time: unsatisfied with some of the tracks he was laying down for the eventually discarded Islands In The Sun album, clearly nervous about being left behind as a 1970s rock dinosaur, looking for a new musical direction, what was more natural than to follow one integral to his early attempts to communicate with his son?

Young has said that the vocoder, with its ethereal, inhuman distortions reminiscent of Sparky's Magic Piano, had allowed him to communicate with Ben, hence the hidden meanings behind a track like Transformer Man, where the computer literally electrifies the listener. If you have any doubts, try playing Transformer Man to a group of small children and watch their faces light up. Amazingly, Like A Hurricane doesn't have the same effect.

The 1980s did mark a massive advance in computer technology in all fields, from air travel and home entertainment (VCRs, video games) to movies and medicine; and Trans, with its own take on an alien yet familiar computer-robot world, is surely influenced by Young's experiences in hospital where so many doctors and paramedics were walking around just so 'this kid could push a button'. As well as the statement of intent that is Computer Age, and the distinctive and personal Transformer Man, Young recorded three other vocoderized tracks for Trans, plus a halfway house retake on Mr Soul in which he sings a synthesized duet with his own natural voice. We R In Control is very much a homage to his old pals from Akron, Ohio, Devo, with its repeated slogans and jerky, rather threatening tempo, by far the least benign take on the invasion of machines. Computer Cowboy (aka Skycrusher) is an oddball, amusing retread of Frankie Laine country and western terrain, reminiscent not only of Young's recent efforts on the soundtrack of the moribund film, *Where The Buffalo Roams*, but of the 1973 mega-hit flick, *Westworld*, with its powerful image of Yul Brynner's animatronic gunslinger on his own route to murderous mayhem. It has one of the funniest moments in the Young canon in its eery, synthesized cowboy chant: 'Come a ky ky yippee yi yippee yi ay'.

But the highlight of this album, which is fatally diluted by some of the remaining tracks, is Sample And Hold, a very fine pop song in its own right, released as a disco 12-inch single with Mr Soul on the reverse, the disco version much heavier on drum machine and bass but with a nice trickle of churning, gruff guitar midway through. Sample And Hold has a superb, instantly catchy riff, heralded by Young's one-string guitar invocation and features some splendidly theatrical vocal interplay on vocoders between Young and Nils Lofgren. Most splendidly, Sample And Hold is a very funny song, dealing with computer dating, not the kind where humans feed names and details into a machine but where the machines are the obscure objects of desire themselves. *'I need a unit to sample and hold,'* Young demands in a dramatically deepened voice, thus showing why the computer sound of Trans is as much about distortion as about clarity, about language as a barrier as much as an avenue of communication.

Young has admitted in interview that at this time he was as interested in hiding his true state of mind behind his music as in revealing it to his fans. In four different versions of this song that I've heard, two recorded, two live, the words change subtly: Young doesn't want an 'angry', 'lonely', lovely', or could it be 'hungry' model; in concert in West Berlin he added 'jealous' to the range of adjectives. And is it a model which 'you desire', 'you designed', or simply 'a new design'? This is a deceptively clever song which reminds me both of Paul Verhoeven's classic film *Robocop* (admittedly not to be released for another five years!) and Bryan Forbes' 1974 *The Stepford Wives*. *'Satisfaction guaranteed in every detail,'* promises Lofgren's dehumanized, angelic voice: *'Please specify/the kind of skin or hide'*. *'We know you'll be happy,'* the manufacturers promise, unconvincingly but sincerely.

There's a paradox here: computerized sound as a perfect musical method, love as a perfect state, but despite the good intentions of all concerned, happiness is unattainable merely through the consumer's specifications. In *Robocop*, Peter Weller's robot law enforcer breaks down when he realizes he has known love and happiness in an earlier human form, and Sample And Hold shows the unbreachable gap between the slick world of technological precision and the complex reality of human relations. That isn't to gainsay its awesome, still potent appeal as an easily addictive piece of early 1980s pop funk.

Sample And Hold was the first of Young's vocoder songs to be performed publicly: at a gig in Palo Alto, California, on 3 August 1982. By the end of the month, Young had embarked on the Transband tour of Europe with a visually bizarre, if musically intriguing, collection of old friends: Ralph Molina from Crazy Horse on drums, Bruce Palmer from Buffalo Springfield on bass and looking like an overweight Parisian boulevardier, complete with jaunty black cap, baggy jeans and a drink problem that caused him to be sacked for part of the tour; Nashville stalwart Ben Keith on pedal steel and Dobro; Californian percussionist Joe Lala and Lofgren, looking exotic, head-scarved and leaping around like a pint-sized hurricane, on guitar. Young hadn't played with him since the Tonight's The Night tour, but though there were suggestions that Young's guitar was drowning Nils', the two and indeed the whole band seemed to get on fine.

The tour swept through France, Italy, Switzerland, Holland, England, Belgium, Norway, Sweden, Denmark and West Germany, often doubling back across borders and finishing with five dates in West Germany, the last one, at Berlin's Deutschlandhalle, being partly recorded for the video, *Neil Young Live In Berlin*. I caught up with the tour at the Wembley Arena on 27 September 1982, and, despite being surprised that Young wasn't including anything from his last two albums on the playlist, I remember it as a successful and well-received concert. Though Young did receive boos on some nights for the new, strange material.

To begin with, he eased the audience in, mixing the old and the new, rock and solo acoustic favourites with vocoder dramatics. Anyway, many of us were too busy clocking the new appearance: Neil Young, by common assent one of rock music's scruffiest performers, in a bright green windbreaker jacket, slacks, a neatly-pressed black shirt and pale pink tie with faded brown diagonal stripes; tall and rangy, his hair was tidy and well-groomed and his face as smooth as a baby's. The new attire was to cause him problems on stage: in Berlin there's a great moment when Neil catches his tie in the strings of his guitar during a stomping solo for Like A Hurricane and responds by tying it around his neck!

It's certain that, just as on the traumatic Tonight's The Night tour, few audience members were acquainted with Young's own set of personal and musical problems at the time, but the rest of the Trans album, plus some discarded outtakes, hint that his brief flirtation with the computer and the vocoder saved his music from blandness and mediocrity: Little Thing Called Love and Hold On To Your Love made it onto Trans, Raining In Paradise and If You've Got Love didn't, but all are very minor stuff, even if the first is catchy enough.

While Neil's change of attire could be explained by the sober realities of meeting men in white coats and tailoring your social routine to the demands of your family, his music obviously needed new challenges. He said at the time that he didn't want to become rock's answer to Perry Como. One of the best moments on the Berlin video is the encore, variously called Berlin or After Berlin and never performed or recorded since. In that, Young sings about not being able to go back to where he started from, and begs us to take him the way he is.

It was a touching end to the tour. Young felt revitalized by playing live after such a long

break; by the mid-1990s he would be accused of touring too much and admitted to an addiction to the live concert experience as the only way to recharge his batteries and connect with ideas and passions. How strange that The Beatles turned in the other direction; how ironic that a tour and an album dominated by artificial sound construction should give Young a taste for the unadulterated, live experience. If the 1980s was Young's wilderness decade and Trans was an album that finally, like the famous curate's egg, was only good in parts, there were still signs here of the regenerations to come.

GET BACK TO THE COUNTRY

First released: Old Ways (Geffen) **August 1985**

Get Back to the Country is hardly the most substantial song on Old Ways but it's the most representative of Young's immersion in country (and sometimes western) music after the brief interlude as a Fifties rocker which produced, in September 1983, a truly ghastly album. Everybody's Rockin' was the creative low-point of Young's career and at around 25 minutes, a sore disappointment to faithful fans who'd taken it to the surprising heights of number 50 in the US album charts and 46 in Britain.

Young's decision to make a full-frontal country roots album, despite the inclusion of the rightly-titled Misfits, an enigmatic cross between Stand By Me and 24 Hours From Tulsa, couldn't have come as a great surprise: his long-time admiration for Frankie Laine, the country singer whose film songs like High Noon, Cool Water and the TV theme for *Rawhide* had given him a huge mass following, was reflected in Young's excellent covers of Laine's The Wayward Wind, which opens Old Ways and contains stirring orchestral overlay that conjures up another of Laine's hits and Young's old faves from his school days, Ghost Riders In The Sky.

For the rest it's a mixture of old-world charm and sugared dreck, featuring contributions from both Willie Nelson and Waylon Jennings and a bevy of female vocalists. The title track reflects the typical and underlying ambivalence of the album: *'Old ways can be a ball and chain,'* sings Neil, both reiterating his passion for traditional music wherein age isn't a problem or a crime and people look after their own, and simultaneously redefining 'old ways' as the perceived excesses of his past rock-star Hollywood life.

Get Back To The Country is a more generous song, a bluegrass reel with Rufus Thibodeaux's fiddle dancing across the basic rhythm section beefed up by piano, banjo, mandolin and Terry McMillan's giggle-making Jew's Harp which sounds inescapably like bedsprings farting. Young's statement of intent couldn't be clearer, a rejection of his younger days for a return to the farm, literally in his case and illustrated on the cover by a backshot of Young in weekend-ranch-hand guise about to disappear down a winding road surrounded by grassy fields and inviting hills. No wonder '*Back in the barn again*' sounds like '*Back in the born again*'.

Young's intentions are clear and had been since June of '84, when he began touring with the International Harvesters, a set-up featuring the Floyd Kramer-style rolling piano of Spooner Oldham and the faithful Ben Keith on steel guitars and vocals – although between February and March 1985, Young was rejoined by Ralph, Molina, Billy Talbot and Frank Sampedro for a tour of New Zealand and Australia. I caught up with this in Memorial Park Drive, Adelaide, on 5 March 1985, and witnessed a bracing set which Young began with Are You Ready For The Country and closed with Get Back To The Country; a rapturous and amusing climax with Young and Anthony Crawford (replacing Thibodeaux on fiddle), cavorting around stage for the instrumental breaks. They then returned for a more conventional set of Crazy Horse-driven evergreens, although Misfits made the list, alongside Cinnamon Girl, Powderfinger and Like A Hurricane.

By the time Old Ways appeared, Young's relationship with Geffen Records had become so fraught that the company was on the point of suing him for producing work 'unrepresentative of Neil Young', which seems truly laughable to anyone who's heard Harvest or Comes A Time.

In retrospect it seems inevitable that company founder David Geffen and Young would clash, both men being entertainment mavericks with their own differing agendas and a clear streak of orneriness. Geffen has always been a man of paradox. He discovered Laura Nyro, was instrumental in relaunching Cher as a solo act and was the executive brain behind John Lennon and Yoko Ono's Double Fantasy released in November 1980, the month before Lennon was so tragically shot. Now openly gay (and benignly philanthropic), he became a billionaire after selling his company in 1990 for ten million shares of MCA stock. When MCA was subsequently bought by the Japanese giant Matsushita, Geffen became a major player in the entertainment industry, big enough to join his pals Steven Spielberg and Jeffrey Katz as the power behind Dreamworks studios and record label.

Yet, even in 1997, Geffen was not past occasional fallings-out with recording artists: Mojo Nixon, a satirical-cowpunker from San Diego, offended the mogul by recording a song called Bring Me The Head Of David Geffen for his ninth album. Nixon told the *Pittsburgh Post Gazette*: 'It just sounded good. They're the ones that re-signed Aerosmith... Instead of giving Aerosmith $80 million, why not give forty bands $2 million? We don't need to hear Aerosmith again – already heard it.' Mojo could have been citing Young when he went on: 'Everybody I know who's been on Geffen, they made them record the record three times. When it comes out, it's a watered-down version of what you liked about it in the first place.'

One of the most curious features of the Old Ways album, recorded largely in Nashville during the spring of 1985, are the excluded tracks which were laid down and seem every bit as good as most of the final selection. One of the most autobiographically engaging is Leaving The Top Forty Behind, where Young makes an easy jest out of his own approaching fortieth birthday and his need to accept his declining position as a rock-star hitmaker.

Like Good Phone and Hillbilly Band, it's a track which carries with it more humour than seems noticeable on Old Ways. The album is doggedly true to a genre that often teeters on the brink and then plunges headlong into maudlin sentimentality and self-obsession.

Young's Amber Jean, recorded at the Castle in Nashville on May 1, has a ringing kinship with the Band's superb Evangeline, sung in tandem with Emmylou Harris, but most regrettable of all perhaps is the neglect of Grey Riders, first heard during an encore at a Harvesters' Chicago gig in August 1985 and described by Alan Jenkins in *Mojo* as 'the anthem of the International Harvesters'. Available only on bootleg, it's a mix of hoe-down and apocalypse, an electrified fence of country and rock influences and far better than absolutely anything on the final Old Ways release.

In summer 1985, as well as playing Live Aid and touring the USA, Young began his long association with Farm Aid after consultations with Bob Dylan and subsequently with Willie Nelson. Young even went to Washington to lobby on behalf of the Farm Policy Reform Act, generally intended to improve the profits and lot of the agricultural community at a time of grave economic crisis which was forcing businesses under in a way reminiscent of John Steinbeck's great novel of the Californian depression, *The Grapes Of Wrath.*

Young must have particularly relished his close association with Willie Nelson, a truly remarkable figure in country music whose rich, pining voice and heartbreaking anthems disguise a wicked sense of humour and a (recent) life spent fighting IRS-induced bankruptcy. Nelson told *Vanity Fair*'s Ron Rosenbaum in November 1991 that, sometime in the early 1980s, he became so addicted to heartbreak songs that made him depressed and started him drinking that he rejected them in a kind of musical cold turkey. So presumably duetting with Young on Are There Any Real Cowboys? was a form of therapy. In the same article, Rosenbaum records an early 1990s breach-of-promise suit involving an LA woman who claimed, among other things, that Nelson had 'made love for nine hours straight in one session, concluding with a spectacular backflip.' 'I'm not saying it didn't happen,' Willie told a reporter, 'but you would have thought I'd remember at least the first four or five hours.'

A friend of mine once interviewed the Texan at home as part of his job as a researcher on a well-known BBC chat show. Nervous and sweating, he asked Willie if it was true that his early life was spent in deep poverty. With the TV camera whirring, Nelson promptly replied: 'Son, we were so poor we had to jerk off the dog in order to feed the cat.' Sadly, and despite many of the finest concerts that Young has taken part in, Farm Aid was cancelled in 1997 for the first time after slow ticket-sales.

THIS NOTE'S FOR YOU

First released: This Note's For You (Reprise) **April 1988**

This Note's For You may be a mere two minutes and four seconds long but that's all it took to transform Neil Young's status among a whole new generation of rock fans; those enthusiasts brought up on a diet of MTV which satisfied their craving for vision-bite babes and streamlined rebellion but also left them a mite hungry and unfulfilled.

Fittingly, This Note's For You can't be separated from its video, directed by England's own Julien Temple (director of Malcolm McLaren's punk history re-write, *The Great Rock And Roll Swindle*), in March 1988. In the space of eighteen months the video was banned by MTV for its 'product placement' – hilarious, given that it was in part a satire on same – and then accepted, shown and finally applauded with MTV's Video Of The Year Award, which Neil received from Daryl Hannah on 6 September 1989.

Though Young branded MTV's executives 'spineless twerps', the irony is that his supposedly radical stance hardly added up to an act of wholesale rebellion. Young decided to go with Temple after seeing his shooting script, which was submitted in advance to MTV. The pair offered to cut out any objectionable material and substitute imagery for a live performance (that wouldn't wash, because of the lyrics) and then even offered to indemnify the company against lawsuits, courtesy of Young's parent record company, Warner.

First, let's fill in the gap between Old Ways and Young's rapturous return to Reprise after a torrid, horrid time at Geffen Records, which culminated with a serious threat of a $3 million law suit. Young released two more albums for Geffen, which superficially appeared to mark a return to his rocking old ways but which add up to little that was either potent or fresh. Both Landing On Water (July 1986) and Life (July 1987) are empty vessels (with the exception of the latter's starkly satirical Mid-East Vacation), and despite an eight-month period of rest and recuperation, the touring schedule that Young and Crazy Horse undertook around this time was fraught and would culminate with his public admission that maybe his once-cherished collaborators didn't have what it took to keep up.

That's not to say that Neil's outings at this time were either unproductive or uneventful: there was the first Bridge Benefit for the Bay Area school which helped children, like his two sons, with learning problems; a reunion with Crosby, Stills and Nash, for their album American Dream, which began recording in April 1987, a year before its release. There was also a hugely enjoyable stint backing Bob Dylan for three dates in June 1988.

By this time, This Note's For You had been released and even those fans and critics still shakin' all over from the memory of The Shocking Pinks gave a largely enthusiastic welcome to his new incarnation as the juke-joint hipster Shakey Deal, the stomping R&B progenitor of 'the dawn of power swing'. This was a New Deal, a man with renewed vigour and flattened, tight, spare blues guitar lines, square-shouldered brass arrangements and liquid horn solos.

According to Pete Long's invaluable guide to Young's concert history, *Ghosts On The Road*, this song was first performed at the Fairweather Post Pavilion in Colombia, Maryland, on 20 August 1987 on a mini-tour with Crazy Horse. On 7 October, Young got a call from manager Elliot Roberts, who told him that the end with Geffen was in sight. Young told *Rolling Stone's*

James Hencke: 'And I had just smoked this big bomber, and I almost had a heart attack. I was so happy, but I was too high to enjoy it.'

From the start, This Note's For You was a massive audience hit: 'Never in my life have I had a song that people reacted to so instantaneously. People just start cheering and singing when we play it. Everybody loves it.'

Young's main targets on the video were fat-cat superstars who, as he sets out over a startling off-key brass-powered riff, '*don't want no cash, don't need no money*'. Which undoubtedly applies to Eric Clapton, Whitney Houston, Michael Jackson, Calvin Klein models and Joe Piscopo, whose endorsements of everything from beer and soft drinks to perfume were mercilessly shredded by Temple. Even '*ain't singing for Spuds*', which I first took to be a reference to potato chips, or crisps, was a swipe at the Budweiser '*booze hound*', Spuds Mackenzie. And to think I'd always wanted to change the line to '*Makes me look like a dud*'. Spuds' lookalike drools all over three female models in a segment that no doubt rang the bells of millions of world-wide would-be Beavis And Buttheads.

On the tastelessness front, 'Whitney' had her wig pulled off and the Michael Jackson ringer had his hair set alight in a replay of the potentially fatal accident that befell the artist currently known as Wacko Jacko. In the august *New York Times*, John Pareles accused Temple, director of megaflop *Absolute Beginners*, of 'toying with homophobia' directed at 'pretty male models' in his send-up of Calvin Klein's Obsession; a product, Pareles noted, wholly unconnected with music. Pareles was both sceptical about Young's intentions and impressed by the result: 'With the juvenile, mean-spirited video clip for that plain-spoken song, Mr. Young just about stripped MTV of its last pretensions to hip irreverence. While the cable channel usually wraps its programming in self-mocking promotion and the knowing smirks of its video jockeys, Mr. Young broke through that irony-clad exterior.'

Amusingly, Neil was later embarrassed when a gig at Golden Hall, San Diego, in October 1988, carried tickets claiming that 'Miller Genuine Draft presents Neil Young'. At Young's suggestion, the theatre management issued a disclaimer that the printing was a mistake and that Neil Young is 'sponsored by nobody'. By then The Bluenotes were no more, changed to Ten Men Workin', named for the opening, sleeves-rolled-up track on this album and after Harold Melvin had filed for an injunction in New York to prevent Young from appropriating the name of his own band, with whom he'd been working since 1970. NY

ORDINARY PEOPLE

Unreleased Recorded: New York, **27 August 1988**

The only unreleased Young song to appear here is a monster at fifteen minutes plus, longer even than Change Your Mind on Sleeps With Angels. It's available on the bootleg double CD, Only Once, taken from a concert by Young and The Bluenotes at the Jones Beach Theatre, Wantaugh, New York, on 27 August 1988. It's well worth getting, especially since Young's long-awaited archive set seems to have been put on the backburner and, Johnny Rogan tells me, may not even appear before Neil's sixtieth birthday.

The song seems to be a particular obsession of Alan Jenkins, who runs *Broken Arrow* fanzine and rates it 'the best unreleased Young tune', particularly since the release of Young's tribute to Steve Stills, Stringman, which appeared on the live Unplugged album. Young has introduced it thus: 'I'm sorry, this song's too long to be on the radio, it's too long to be a video, it's probably too long to be on a record. But we keep on finding it and it keeps us going.'

Young was probably more concerned about radio play: artists from The Grateful Dead to Bob Dylan have released whole album sides with just one track and Young has recorded his debt to jazzman John Coltrane (see Love To Burn), whose whole recording career was predicated on the increased freedom that came with the LP record. Sadly, Young ditched this from the album and from an abandoned project of concert material to have been called This Note's For You Too. A main criticism of This Note's For You was the limitations of the songs, which included Sunny Inside from 1982, and Ain't It The Truth, a primitive R&B standard dating back to the Canadian 1960s.

For Ordinary People, Young's guitar rises in classic Robert Cray style against a cascade of falling horns led by Steve Lawrence's tenor, Larry Cragg's baritone and Tommy Bray's trumpet. It's a ten-verse full-scale epic, covering everything from Wild West showdowns to hot-rod racers to crime bosses 'at the window with a big cigar', to dispossessed factory hands, antique dealers, vigilantes, gunmen, the homeless, drug dealers, government agents, unemployed models, defeated boxers, Las Vegas highrollers, drunks and railroad operatives (old trains were a big passion of Young's). All of them are in their own ways Ordinary People. The images are as startling and detailed as Blonde On Blonde-era Dylan.

Only the urban-conscious Life In The City, in which Young sings of *'people sleeping on the sidewalks on a rainy day/families livin' under freeways/it's the American way,'* comes within light years of the power and energy on display here. The barrelhouse frenzy between the bass-and-drums-led verses seems to mix Elmore James, Cray and Joe Louis Walker with Freddie King and Wes Montgomery, making this the best and most authentic electric blues Young has ever played. The subject matter makes this Young's own attempt at the song equivalent of John Dos Passos's epic novel, *USA*.

Absurdly, this unashamedly populist number has been accused of having fascist undertones in its supposed call to the instincts of the mob. But the song, which does, after all, say of ordinary folk that 'some are saints, some are jerks', reminds me more of the great American maverick campaigner Michael Moore, whose movie *Roger And Me* detailed his attempts to confront the General Motors executive who shut down the plant in his hometown of Flint, Michigan. Moore's wonderful *TV Nation* is an engaging mixture of radicalism and irreverence which has proved,

among other things, that a black superstar has more trouble hailing a New York cab than a white convicted murderer. While Moore is always the champion of the little guy against the corporations or the politicians, so Young's song rousingly affirms the dignity of the common man and woman, the dignity of honest toil, the suffering of those '*living in a nightmare*' who are going to bring the good things back'. And if the song were about stamp-collecting there'd still be that piercing, juddering guitar and those hair-raising horns. NY

ROCKIN' IN THE FREE WORLD

First released: Freedom (Reprise) **October 1989**

It's almost as if Neil Young planned the whole thing. Just as he ended the 1970s with the glories of Rust Never Sleeps, so he finished off the 1980s in which he'd seemingly meandered through techno, rockabilly, country, garage rock, art rock and blues with the aptly-named Freedom. It was his best-selling album for ten years and so praised that it garnered Rolling Stone's only five-star review of 1989.

Like Rust, Freedom opens and closes with two versions of an anthem, one live and acoustic, the other studio and electric. For My My, Hey Hey and its closing variant read Rockin' In The Free World. While the former examined the contrasting pulls on the rock star towards survival or destruction, so Rockin' played with the ironies of the album's title in the wake of the collapse of communism and the horrors of Tiananmen Square, which made the West feel so smug and superior. Geoffrey Himes' review in *The Washington Post* was acutely perceptive: 'If freedom of housing means "people sleepin' in their shoes", if freedom of opportunity means Latin American drug smuggling and crack selling on Broadway, if romantic freedom means "someone else will sleep with tears", if entrepreneurial freedom means "Styrofoam boxes for the ozone layer", what kind of freedom is it?'

Freedom took eighteen months to complete and is one of his most lovingly produced. It evolved from yet another aborted project, Times Square, a return to crunchy electronics and growling feedback which the artist considered just too uncommercial. Instead, five tracks became a mini-album called Eldorado only released in Japan and Australasia for an accompanying tour. In the end, Freedom was a triumphant compromise, with six songs from Times Square, five other compositions, two of which, The Ways Of Love and Too Far Gone, dated from the mid-1970s, plus an outrageously deranged reworking of Lieber and Stoller's 1963 hit for the Drifters and, later, George Benson, On Broadway. The composers weren't over-impressed: Mike Stoller told me bluntly that he 'preferred the original'.

The acoustic Rockin' is an edited version of a performance at Jones Beach on 14 June 1989, during a short solo tour in which Young astonished audiences not only with his new, no-nonsense, leather-jacketed presence but with the volume and ferocity of his acoustic playing. For this date, he was joined by Bruce Springsteen for an encore of Down By The River and it's easy to see the Springsteen influence in Young's new-found urban angst; in fact, Young has acknowledged the song's links to Born In The USA.

Young, a man who had indulged in marijuana happily enough, was clearly rattled by the threat of drugs like crack and cocaine, particularly to his own children, Zeke having encountered the problem at school first-hand. And like Springsteen, Young, the former vocoder king, knew that true rock music was about toil, tears and sweat. No wonder he told Edna Gundersen of *USA Today*: 'maybe the music of the 1990s will bring back the rhythm of humanity and not the rhythm of a computer'. With This Note's For You and Freedom, Young had introduced new material that was good enough to stop people screaming for the oldies. Young told Gundersen from the comfort of his estate-sized, log-fired ranch near San Francisco: 'Remember when you used to watch TV in the '60s and you'd see Perry Como in a

NUCLEAR
MARTIN

cashmere sweater? That's what rock 'n' roll is becoming. It's your parents' music.'

No small irony that he was finding acolytes among a new generation of rocksters who aped his torn jeans and faded plaid shirts, his pulled-across-a-mountain-range-backwards hair, and whose respect led to the tribute album The Bridge released so close to Freedom that *Rolling Stone* reviewed them in tandem. It was conceived by Young enthusiast Terry Tolkin, who committed part of the proceeds to the Bridge School project and, despite the occasional dud, it's a recording that anticipates Young's new-found rawness. As *Rolling Stone*'s reviewer, David Fricke, noted: 'the garage-punk disembowelling' of Young's techno tracks Lotta Love and Computer Age by, respectively, Dinosaur Jr and Sonic Youth make Young's treatment of On Broadway seem quite restrained'. It also carried a slow and solemn version of Helpless *a la* Nico by Nick Cave, the Pixies' wonderfully turned-on Winterlong and Don't Let It Bring You Down by southern songstress Victoria Williams and the Williams Brothers. Neil was happy but not entirely: with his recognizable combination of grudge and grunge he muttered about 'not being ready to be embalmed'. The opposite was the case: Rockin' In The Free World has been covered as much as any post-1970s song: versions exist by The Alarm (the best), Big Country, Bryan Adams, Icicle Works, Van Halen, David Byrne and, of course, Pearl Jam.

Young's storming electrified closer adds another verse with a more political flavour, singing about 'a kinder, gentler machine-gun hand', but it's the song's bleakness, cutting right through the deliberately catchy cliché of the hook-line which gives the song its special appeal. Little can be added to the line which describes the horrors of the street junkie way of life: *'That's one more kid who will never go to school/Never get to fall in love/Never get to be cool.'*

For more humorous takes on the glibness of the Free World (sic) see not only The Beatles' mischievous Chuck Berry parody Back In The USSR from The White Album but also Leonard Cohen's Democracy (Has Come To The USA) from his truly great 1992 release, The Future – proof that Neil Young isn't the only ageing Canadian with brains, balls and a song to sing. NY

CRIME IN THE CITY & ELDORADO

First released: Freedom (Reprise) **October 1989**

There's not a single bad track on Freedom, so it's hard to have to pass over other choice cuts: the explosive feedback frenzy of Don't Cry, with Young's whiningly assertive vocal playing over a tune that sounds like it's running backwards; the retro bar-hound humour of Too Far Gone, with acoustic and mandolin playing a jaunty double take on the self-deprecatory narrative; the gentle piano-led fatalism of Wrecking Ball, later to be wrecked by Emmylou Harris on an over-produced Daniel Lanois album foray; Linda Ronstadt's gorgeous vocal harmonies on Hangin' On A Limb and The Ways Of Love; or Someday, where Steve Lawrence's tenor soars, like '*Rommel in his plane*'.

These songs are the true highlights of the record: Eldorado, already legendary from the import mini-album which *Melody Maker* considered as fine as any rock guitar playing ever laid down, even though two of the most startling tracks, Cocaine Eyes and Heavy Love, never made the Freedom cut; and Crime In The City, a six-verse reduction of the Bluenotes classic, Sixty To Zero.

Both are highly accomplished musical excursions: Eldorado a brooding combination of electric guitar, Spanish acoustic played by 'Poncho Villa' (or Frank Sampedro) and maracas subtly punctuating the melody; Crime In The City a driving rocker with Young's voice rarely more intense or pleading. Both are movies or movie fragments: Eldorado yet another Young song imbued with the search for 'gold', a Sergio Leone western turning into Sam Peckinpah, with a Mexican setting and a drugs deal going down to the accompaniment of mariachi bands, tolling mission bells, a blues guitar that *'echoes in the alleyway'* and the swish of gorgeous women *'all dressed in diamonds and sables'*. Then the last verse switches to Hemingway mode: a homage to the bullfighter with eyes of *'screaming blue'* and hair as *'red as blood'*, a survivor and a hero who *'lives to fight another day'*. It's a song with no beginning or end, the film you produce in your head with a free soundtrack.

Crime In The City is a cop show, a saga of corruption and disillusionment, starting with a bank heist that soon becomes the stuff of exploitation TV and ending with the story of a 'fireman', literally, perhaps, or even the metaphorical kind who's brought in to sort out trouble, legal or otherwise. The man ends up in prison for life without parole; the crime is unnamed but the man wishes he'd never put down his hose, *'wish I'd never got old'*. As rugged as the best Springsteen, it's a particularly brilliant example of Young's lyric writing: each verse is fifteen lines long (sixteen if you count the 'yeahs') and exceptional on spoken word.

Like all the best movies, the song is driven by character and case history. Both are tragic figures: the cop who gets paid by a ten-year-old, which could mean either street bribes or just the fact that he's stayed on the beat too long, an unpromoted figure now forced to rub shoulders with his juniors; and the fireman who once saved lives and had control but who's now a broken man. Breaking up these two scenarios is a verse about a product of a broken home, a stanza some have taken to be a reference to Neil's own experience of his parents' split. However, unlike Neil's background in rural Canada, the kid's position is unexceptional. This is an exceptional song on a superb album, a song that aches for De Niro, Pacino or Duvall and a screenplay by Tarantino, Joe Esterhaus or Paul Schrader. NY

LOVE TO BURN

First released: Ragged Glory (Reprise) **September 1990**

If any Neil Young album needs volume it's Ragged Glory, which saw him starting the 1990s on a high-octane surge, basking in the reception of Freedom, dubbed 'The Godfather Of Grunge' and the only begetter of the garage-rock new wave dominated by the Seattle sounds of Nirvana, Pearl Jam, Soundgarden and Alice In Chains. Odd that some British critics had wallowed in thoughts of the coming rock apocalypse after the break-up of The Smiths.

Young now had the clout and the confidence to recall his old war nags Crazy Horse, who had been in exile since the fraught times of 1986-87 and two of whom, bassist Talbot and drummer Molina, had something to prove, although to hear them banging on about each other to Jim Jarmusch in 1996 you'd sometimes think they'd never had a parting of the ways in their lives. Young summoned the trio to his wide-open-spaced ranch and began work on Ragged Glory in June-July 1990. By this time, his home not only had a fully-equipped, state-of-the-art recording studio with on-line editing facilities, but a full-sized open air stage on which most of this music was made, during balmy summer evenings, using the old faithfuls of booze, smokes (legal) and old-boy fun, in a series of mostly one-take, high-volume excursions into touchy-feely and occasionally off-key-ly vintage rock. You can largely forget the lyrics and the sentiments here: *Musician* praised Young for returning to the eternal verities, but what does he say about them? Love and idealism are good. Betrayal and bullshit are bad. Cor!

What makes Ragged run is its music; raw, greasy, a dishwater shower of excitement, speed, muscle and testosterone. And, hey, guys and gals, it was made by the man who gave us Comes A Time and Harvest. Who cares that its spiritual centre seems to be the gross Don't Spook The Horse, left off the album but released on a CD single and as obsessed with excrement as anything written by the author of *Gulliver's Travels*? Who cares that the accompanying video showed curvy female farm-hands waggling their butts in cut-away jeans to Farmer John? After all, it always seemed to work for ZZ Top. The boys were back on the ranch.

There was a certain opportunism behind the venture. Young knew the potential of such an album and recognized that Crazy Horse, with whom he's built up a musical ESP that lasts to this day, was the best vehicle. But given the experiments of the 1980s, we can be thankful he didn't follow Freedom with a foray into acid house, hip-hop or a white rap album in the style of Public Enemy. Whatever the reasoning behind Ragged, the proof of the pudding is in the devouring: forget the haste with which the tracks were laid down, or the seemingly random bunch of songs which lurch from the mid-1970s (White Line, Country Home) back to the Squires days (Farmer John) and touch on the hippy-trippy 1960s (Mansion On The Hill, Days That Used To Be).

Love To Burn, along with Love And Only Love, is over ten minutes long. And while the closer, Mother Earth, which combines Jimi Hendrix guitar pyrotechnics with a melody taken from the traditional ballad And Both Shall Row (My Love and I), is a live take as fine as anything on the album. Love To Burn is the best example of extended power playing here and on the later live tour collection, Weld. It also seems a good place to examine Young's links with the great jazz saxophonist, John Coltrane.

The ever-perceptive Nick Kent asked Young about the Coltrane link in a 1995 *Mojo* interview with special reference to this album. Young said 'my guitar improvisations with Crazy Horse are very, very Coltrane-influenced. I'm particularly taken by work like Equinox and My Favourite Things.' He also nodded to Miles Davis, but more generally to 'his overall attitude towards the concept of "creation", which is one of constant change'.

Given that Young is the master of the three-chord rock riff and Crazy Horse the masters of the steady, pounding rock beat, it's an unlikely connection. Cop this quote from JC Thomas's authoritative Coltrane study, *Chasing The Trane*, attributed to Martin Williams: *'Coltrane could superimpose a world of passing chords, substitute chords and harmonic extensions upon a harmonic structure that was already complex. And at times he seems to be prepared to gush out every possible note, find his way step by step through every complex chord, in which a note could be 'cracked' to reveal another world of pitches hidden within, rising up thye harmonic series, careen through every scale and go beyond even that profusion by groping for impossible notes and sounds in a tenor saxophone that seemed ready to shatter under the strain.'* Blimey.

Coltrane was a master of 'harmonics' which you can demonstrate by striking the bottom C of a piano hard: the note will resonate through a series of octaves. Coltrane was obsessed with his instrument as a physical entity: his playing exhibited a ferocity, speed and sheer muscle-power which leaves most practitioners of the horn humbled to this day. The term 'sheets of sound', which was coined by the critic Ira Gitler for Trane and which Jim Jarmusch has applied to Young's playing with Crazy Horse on the 1996 world tour, is an attempt to improvize at break-neck speed, playing every available note in a chord, even in compositions where the changes may come every two beats. Coltrane would honk and holler into his mouthpiece, he would shake and sway with the instrument, be it soprano or tenor, just as Hendrix and Young himself would shake their guitars to bend notes, or violently strike their strings, or pound them on the floor, or pluck at them with their teeth, or ram them masturbatorily against the amps. Coltrane would play off the metal of his horn, making all kinds of 'illegitimate' noises, just as Young has more than dabbled in the use of feedback noise: on the Ragged Glory video he can be seen ramming his headstock into a toilet bowl, which he aptly dismissed as 'Hollywood shit', and, like Jimmy Page, has been known to experiment in echo-friendly bathrooms.

Coltrane's own experiments were groundbreaking. In the late 1950s, on While My Lady Sleeps, he executed a breathtaking trick on the last three-note chord, splitting his note in half, like an atom. At the time of Impressions and My Favourite Things, he was obsessed with making sense of the sounds in his head, a master of aggressive overblowing who cracked notes like a prize fighter, producing ragged chords. By the end of his short life, and even after the rapture of the spiritual A Love Supreme, Coltrane had recorded Interstellar Space with Rashied Ali his sole accompanist on drums and was pushing his sax to its limit, playing so fast that he was creating 'fluke sounds', extra notes from the mouthpiece's harmonics. It was recorded in 1967, around the same time that John Lennon was insisting that he'd originated electronic feedback on I Feel Fine.

On Love To Burn, we can start to see the newfound intensity of Crazy Horse's playing with Young, which was to find even greater extension on Sleeps With Angels, The Complex Sessions and The Year Of The Horse. Chords are dissected, ripped apart; improvisations are layered and challenging, not repeating notes or sequences but using them to build whole new structures; and the collective spirit of the band, no small thanks to Sampedro's awesomely powerful rhythm lines, plucked from the fattest strings in the biz, recall the speed and sheer audacity of Coltrane's extraordinary flights, notably his soprano playing on My Favourite Things, in which the instrument just refuses to die down. At this time, Young bewailed the lack of any real jamming in rock music, musicians like Billy Gibbons and Mark Knopfler limited by their commerciality, Eric Clapton boring all but the diehard blues faithful with two hours plus of annual blues at the Albert Hall. Right up to the slow-burn feedback fade-out, Love To Burn is a tribute to the scale of Captain Crank-Up's revival.

The lyrics aren't bad either, offering a stark dissection of a marriage gone wrong, the lovers' conversation, both accusatory and full of pity. This is a 45-year-old man who could take

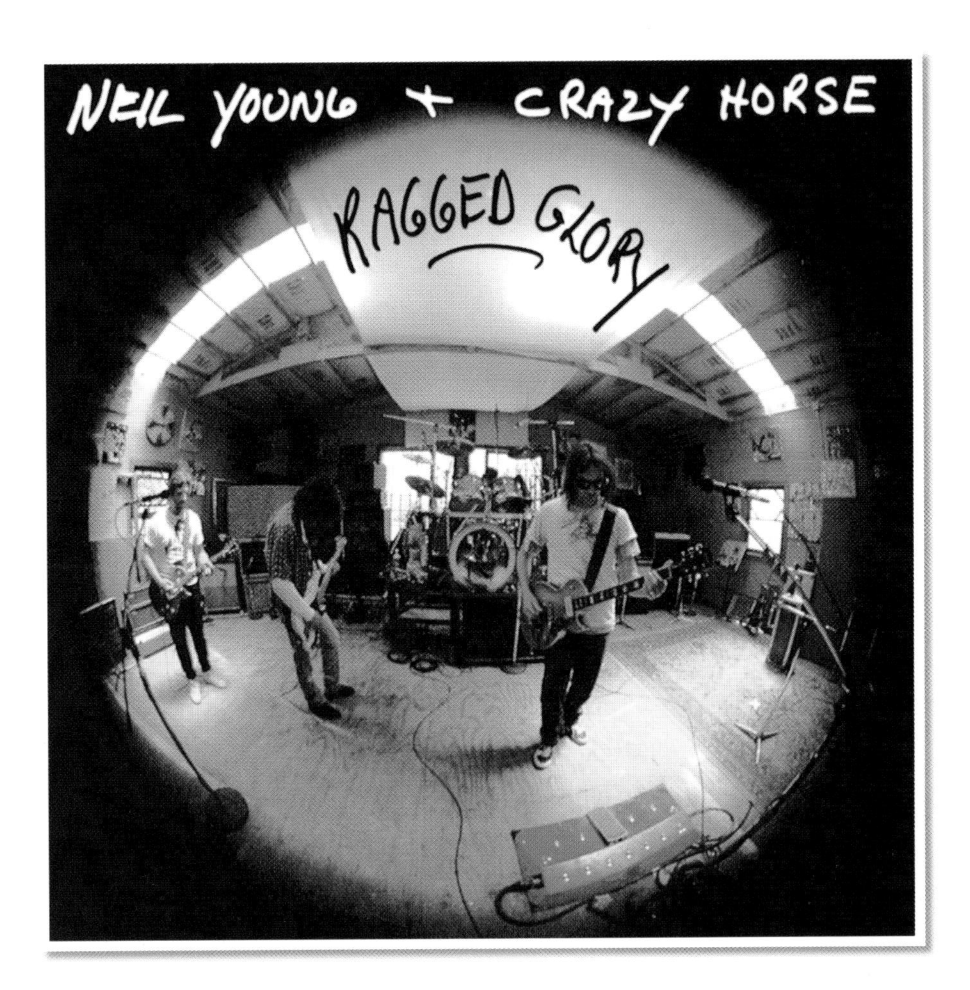

'boring' out of the term, 'boring old fart'. Young was to take his feedback experiments to the edge with Arc, a bonus CD of unashamed noise which, he told *Musician* in 1991, was like the movie *Fantastic Voyage*, where doctors reduce themselves to the size of microbes to operate on a seriously ill bigshot; 'like a trip through a power chord. The chord may last like five or six seconds but it takes 35 minutes at the size we're reducing ourselves to go through it. To me, Arc is more art and expression than anything I've done in a long time.' Yeah, and to me, it's still a great way of getting rid of unwanted guests. NY

FROM HANK TO HENDRIX

First released: Harvest Moon (Reprise) **November 1992**

After a gruelling 53-date, four-week tour with the Crazies, Neil found himself with hearing problems serious enough for him to tone down the volume and substitute a series of short, acoustic-based dates to promote his next album. Another appealing irony: Harvest was in part the product of back trouble and two decades later its putative follow-up was due to tinnitus, a chronic condition which leads to ringing in the ears and is the curse of rockers everywhere. It also afflicted my late mother, who never stood next to an amplifier in her life.

Harvest Moon was a big jump from Ragged Glory and Arc/Weld, though Young told *Musician*: 'Everybody's been asking me to do this for years, and I'd go: "Well, I don't feel it. I don't wanna do it." But after I did Arc and took it so far out there, I wrote these songs and I looked at 'em and said: "Oh my God, there it is." It's with The Stray Gators, the same band I used on Harvest. It's gonna be beautiful and we start cutting in two days.'

Well, it was The Stray Gators plus the Muscle Shoals might of Spooner Oldham's piano, and old faces like Ronstadt, Larson and James Taylor,. Young told Ben Thompson of the *Independent On Sunday* in 1994: 'It's an album of songs about hanging on and trying to make things last, and being able to reach back into the past and take it with you, rather than having to abandon it.'

From Hank To Hendrix isn't as musically remarkable as the closer Natural Beauty (yet again a live track with overdubs, recorded in Portland, Oregon) but it represents the spirit of the record better than any, certainly better than the overrated title track which Young never performs well in concert and which sounds like the Everly Brothers on Horlicks.

It was first performed at the Fifth Bridge Benefit on 2 November 1991, during a short set with The Gators which was the meat in the sandwich, the bread of which was provided by the opening duets with Larson and Nils Lofgren and the closing rendition of Henry VIII's chart-topping Greensleeves with Willie Nelson. It begins on a disarmingly soft, lilting curve, Young's harmonica blending sublimely with a muted accordion and Ben Keith's ever-evocative pedal steel. The song begins like a CV or report card. It's both a job description and a tribute to three of Young's biggest influences: the immortal Hendrix, with whom Young once stole a pick-up truck outside Woodstock; and to two Hanks, Marvin and Williams. Marvin's influence, present since Young's teens, can always be seen in the vigorous use of the tremolo arm during Young's solos. And while Young has never, to my knowledge, recorded a Hank Williams song, he does own his old Martin-D28 and plays it regularly. He bought it from Tut Taylor and told *Guitar Player* in March 1992: 'It's always great when someone understands about what this is they're holding, who understands the effect Hank Williams had over all of us.'

It's uncertain whether Young wrote any of these songs on this guitar, but he does believe that an instrument can improve an artist's creative chances. The tributes in this song also include Marilyn Monroe and Madonna, a span of five decades, and its sweep is widened further by the change from homage to unease. *'I didn't believe in much, but I believed in you.'* In what? In the power of music, of friendship? In the woman to whom the song seems to be addressed, with whom he's heading for the 'big divorce'? Surely not wife Pegi, to whom the album is dedicated?

It's one of his most feminine albums, and the woman is a universal image of succour and support, forbearance and love. *'The same things that make you live/Can kill you in the end.'* This fine ellipsis runs from the drug deaths of Danny Whitten and Bruce Berry to Hendrix's own bizarre and pitiful demise, to the thirst for success, the naked ambition which Young has never denied has always been part of his make-up. The song One Of These Days talks of burying hatchets, of writing to old friends, healing old wounds. But then Young has done better out of life than, say, David Crosby. Sitting on top of the pile, he no doubt felt like looking back without anger for the same reason that dogs lick their balls: because he could. But as this song suggests, with its ambivalent note of renewal and change, of time passing and people changing, life can be a signing-off as well as a chance to revisit the past.

On 10 January, Young jammed with a galaxy of guitar heroes at the 1992 Hall Of Fame Concert in New York – among them U2's The Edge, Steve Cropper, Keith Richard, BB King and Hendrix's bassist Noel Redding. He performed Hendrix's Purple Haze and the Dylan-Hendrix song All Along The Watchtower. Whatever it did for his hearing, he repeated the latter triumphantly at the Bobfest, the Dylan Tribute Concert at Madison Square Gardens on 16 October. Young's rather dismissive behaviour to the tearful Sinead O'Connor, who left the stage after an anti-Catholic rant, seemed almost amusing. Who was that nutty broad? He was hailed for his set, playing with Booker T And The MGs and using Watchtower as a bracing set-closer on their subsequent tour.

There's another version available on a double CD set that was originally released to radio stations only, a part of the Farm Aid Seven concert at the New Orleans Superdome on 18 September 1994. Sadly, however, it's all but wrecked by Willie Nelson's flailing, out-of-place acoustic backup. NY

CHANGE YOUR MIND

First released: Sleeps With Angels (Reprise) **September 1994**

While Harvest Moon reached number twelve in the UK, his highest British chart position since Christ was a carpenter, Young's next studio album, Sleeps With Angels, came into the Billboard ranks at number nine. Sleeps With Angels has many undertones of Tonight's The Night and is certainly his most unsettling and arresting collection since its release in 1975. The albums are connected by a number of factors: Los Angeles, where they were recorded; the speed of their recording, which amounted to no more than a couple of weeks; and their deathly contexts, for Tonight the drug deaths of Danny Whitten and Bruce Berry, and the suicide by gunshot of Nirvana leader Kurt Cobain for Sleeps. Young not only admired Cobain and had tried to talk him through several depressions, but Cobain had quoted Young's lines about burning out being preferable to fading away in his last note *(see entry for My My, Hey Hey)*. There was another fatality surrounding the album, the drive-by killing of a woman friend of the band's, and the mood of sombreness couldn't have been lightened by the throat cancer of Booker T bass player Donald 'Duck' Dunn, which aborted plans for an album with the band with whom he'd toured so successfully in 1993. And while Tonight's The Night was the first studio recording after Harvest, this strange masterpiece followed on from its supposedly mellow successor.

Both 1994 deaths are marked by album tracks: the title song, whose opening was described by David Toop in *The Times* as like 'the starting grid at a monster truck race' and whose sentiment '*too late, too soon*', recalls the sentiments of '*tonight's the night*'. It's a strangely dispassionate take on Cobain's death, though, and if you didn't know that it was about the musician and his widow Courtney Love the song would give you no clue, something reviewers seem to have skipped over. Drive-by is more elegiac, with starry images recalling the lyrics of Someday from Freedom and a quirky acoustic lead that seems to have picked up where that album left off.

Sleeps With Angels is, as I've said, a disturbing album, not only imbued with sadness but oddly displaced, almost a kind of musical 'creepy-crawlying' , the way in which Charles Manson's family members would unsettle a victim by breaking into their home and slightly rearranging the furniture. Arrangements here aren't simple or obvious: Prime Of Life has a bizarrely dreadful flute played by Frank Sampedro which is so ghastly that it sounds like a three-year-old with a Xmas present; the beautiful opener My Heart utilizes a ghostly combination of marimbas and saloon-bar 'tack' piano, although this song has been ruined for me by my son's (accurate) observation that it sounds like something Kermit The Frog would serenade the Muppets with; Train Of Love and Western Hero utilize the same rhythm tracks and still manage to sound unconventional; the ear-whacking off-key harmonica on A Dream That Can Last. Crazy Horse take the hint as well, Talbot's drumming sounding variously like Keith Moon on pig's adrenaline, a fragment from an Orange Day parade, or understated and jazzy.

Change Your Mind is the musical centrepiece of this record and at nearly fifteen minutes the longest studio track Young has ever put down. On 3 October, Young and Crazy Horse played a live, undubbed studio set hours after an acclaimed benefit for the Bridge School, and this song comes in at almost the same length in a 27-minute classic filmed by Jonathan Demme as The Complex Sessions and including three other songs from the album; Prime Of Life (minus flute), My Heart

and Piece Of Crap (Young ends by breaking a string after Crap and the Complex version has an extra two lines about his pet hatred, digitalized sound).

Unlike Harvest Moon, Neil remained taciturn about this album, refusing to do interviews or promotions, and the label issued various spin-offs to compensate, including an almost unprecedented trio of CD singles, one containing two versions of this monster, the album track and a 5:17-minute radio edit. There was also a cassette version with Speaking Out as a B-side.

Change Your Mind has obvious links with all the great Neil Young guitar explorations, notably Like A Hurricane, Down By The River and Cowgirl In The Sand. It's certainly no thrasher, although Chris Heath may have been a little harsh when he called it in *Mojo*: 'Fifteen minutes of loping grunge-fest punctuated by the sort of gloriously lazy guitar doodles which loiter so magnificently and slothfully that you can almost hear Neil Young's sideburns growing as he considers moving a finger.' What some might call laziness seems mysterious, ethereal, deliberately laboured, like the song itself, which is an exploration of marriage, the life force which gives Sleeps its light side, a celebration of a state that Young seems to be trying to understand, not just through the shifting patterns and tones of his guitar work but by his voice, which pours out a succession of marital mantras. Any attempt to analyse it through them is doomed, however, as Young changes the lyrics on all four versions of this that I've heard: 'supporting you' can become 'rejecting you' at will, and the two can hardly be reconciled. The lyrics aren't helped by the inclusion of 'odour' to apply to the fragrance of a bedroom in which 'more than a million roses bloom'. One is reminded ineluctably of farts beneath the bedclothes. NY

SAFEWAY CART

First released: Sleeps With Angels (Reprise) **September 1994**

The recording history between Harvest Moon and Sleeps reflected Young's new status: a highly-praised and commercially successful video and CD, Unplugged, recorded at a MTV concert and most notable for the pump-organ Like A Hurricane and the final unveiling of Stringman, his paean to Stephen Stills. There was also Lucky Thirteen, an over-ambitiously-titled attempt by Geffen to capitalize on the man's rebirth by collecting the best of his stuff for the label during the 1980s.

Some critics had started to bridle at Young's apparent ability to do no wrong: in the *Observer*, Caroline Sullivan somewhat churlishly reminded fans that Young had once supported Reagan and Ross Perot, although even she admitted that his twenty-eighth solo album since 1969 merited some of the greatest accolades of the last five years. Safeway Cart is a highlight of the album, an onomatopoeic song in which sound reinforces content. In his wonderful essay on this album, collected in *Love To Burn: Thirty Years Of Speaking Out*, Paul Williams calls it 'a masterpiece'. The combination of instruments and beat add up to an unearthly urban churn: a wailing fuzz-box harmonica that screeches like a train whistle, Sonny

Boy Williamson meets the J Geils Band, a left hand flat-stick drum march, a trudging two-note guitar riff and a bass line that sounds like some gruff heartbeat. It adds up to a direct counterblast at the opening image, or rather the opening simile, for this is a song which is *'like a Safeway cart rolling down the street'*.

But this isn't a rolling shopping trolley, this is a cart being pushed uphill by a Sisyphus with back trouble. This is a clearly placed song about urban decay and isolation, a song about LA down-and-outs, the kind of folk who push their possessions in mobile wire cages across freeways and down the middle of roads roaring with speeding cars. LA is a town where even the racist jokes have a motorized theme: 'What do you get if you cross a Mexican with a Korean?' 'A car thief who can't drive'. As Williams asks brilliantly: 'aren't these people "invisible"?' What do we notice most, the trolley or the human being behind it? The cardboard box or the kid squatting inside?

Like Young's punky Piece Of Crap, this is a condemnation of consumerist values but it's more evocative and all-embracing, like looking at a telescope through the wrong end, a song which plants the footprint of Christ in the soulless mall or charts the progress of social rejects through the simple image of '*the sandal mark on the Saviour's feet*'. The song also combines imagery of imprisonment and abandonment with sounds of travel and work; the Safeway Cart, like so much on this album, could be a homage to the train, one of Young's real passions, while the piercing harp is both a railroad whistle and a factory siren, echoes of past economic boom times, written even before today's 'welfare' situation where hard-working, long-employed folk can find themselves on the streets after just weeks of unemployment.

The song comes to no conclusion because it's a 'like' song: Young almost whispers the lyrics, as if he's trying not to wake the undead, the 'baby' who '*looks so bad with her TV eyes/going, going, gone, and the picture cries*', more references to Christianity, perhaps, in the image of the weeping Madonna, which could also be merely more MTV dreck. This is a song about need: surprising right to the end, with its burst of trumpet and almost inaudible flute which comes in at the fade. It also loosens up gradually after the taut, anguished opening, almost like someone with a blocked-up nose finally succeeding in clearing those airways. This is serious stuff, even if the guy once did say some nice things about Reagan. NY

ACT OF LOVE

First released: Mirror Ball (Reprise) **June 1995**

Neil Young is surely unique in having produced rock masterpieces in each of the four decades since the 1960s, albeit leaving it very late with Everybody Knows This Is Nowhere (1969) and Freedom (1989). After the off-centre glories of Sleeps With Angels, he was to step sideways with Mirror Ball, a collaboration with Seattle post-grungers Pearl Jam. The outfit comprised founder members Jeff Ament (bass) and Stone Gossard (guitar), former Red Hot Chili Peppers drummer Jack Irons, Mike McCready (lead guitar) and vocalist Eddie Vedder. And at the time of their team-up with Young Pearl Jam were much more than just a younger version of Crazy Horse. Two of their albums, VS and Vitalogy, had topped the US charts, and their anti-establishment stance, notably cancelling concerts in protest at the pricing practices of Ticketmaster, obviously struck a ragged chord with Young. The band had even had its own brush with the reaper when founding vocalist Andrew Wood, born in 1966, the year Buffalo Springfield were formed, died of a heroin overdose in March 1990.

Though rumours of Young teaming up with bands from Nirvana to Sonic Youth had circulated for some time, Pearl Jam were the obvious choice, particularly since they had turned Rockin' In The Free World into their own concert anthem. Such an alliance seemed inevitable as early as December 1993, when the highly-respected *Musician* magazine named 'Neil Young and Pearl Jam' as their band of the year on the back of a few tour encores and an appearance at the MTV awards when they combined for Rockin' In The Free World. *Musician* enthused: 'Fierce, fearless and exuberant in the way the best rock 'n' roll always appears to be, Young seemed to find in Pearl Jam a spark of his younger self, and Pearl Jam might have found in Young a star to steer by.'

In 1994, Young was nominated for an Academy Award for his title song for the film *Philadelphia* and played at the ceremony, even though he was beaten by buddy Bruce Springsteen's Streets Of Philadelphia, written for the same film. In early October that year, he played two Bridge School benefits with Crazy Horse for which Pearl Jam appeared and encored with Young on the grunge-punk Piece Of Crap. But Act Of Love is the song that really kick-started their recording relationship, which was also helped when Young stood in for Vedder on some dates when the singer went down with a sore throat.

Act Of Love was first played live with Crazy Horse on 12 January 1995, when Young was finally inducted into the Rock 'N' Roll Hall Of Fame, three years after he'd jocularly called for it to be closed down! The induction was performed by Vedder and two weeks later Young, Crazy Horse and Pearl Jam combined to perform Act Of Love as an encore at the Voters For Choice benefit in Washington DC. In later January and early February, the Rock Godfather made the Jam an offer they couldn't refuse and two two-night sessions ensued at the Bad Animals studio in Seattle, teaching them a series of new songs as they went along.

How did they differ from Crazy Horse? asked Steve Morse of the *Minneapolis Star Tribune*: 'They play more tough and steady... Crazy Horse is really dynamic. Their sound goes way up and way down. But the songs I've written for Pearl Jam are right-on-through kind of songs... They share a certain rawness... I think they're older than I am in some ways.

They don't sound or play young.' He could have also noted the almost total lack of the signature Horse backing vocals.

Whether Mirror Ball was a righteous coming together of prophet and disciples or another slick marketing ploy, the whole spirit of the record is a marriage between earnest rock aggression and a kind of po-faced, retrospective hippy idealism. Even more than Ragged Glory, it was also another example of Young's search for raw, anti-studio anti-refinement. It was put together in less than a week without much in the way of warm-ups, rehearsals or even tunings-up: amusingly, after Downtown you can hear Young saying: 'Well, we know that one... it's funky,' a strange comment to make about a final version, but again in keeping with an album that is spattered with impromptu remarks to add to the let's-do-the-show-right-here feel. And as such it has its limitations: the intensity and originality of Sleeps gives way to of-the-moment jamming, with the inevitable assortment of missed changes, bum notes and mistimed vocal parts. But Young, now approaching 50, still had his rock boots on, and was still willing and able to (literally) engage in inter-generational dialogue.

By the mid-1990s, the anti-abortion backlash had begun to peak: witness such disparate phenomena as the comments of influential newspaper columnists, campaigns by the born again and the Catholic right wing, the direct action factions that had murdered doctors in Florida and the South, even the well-publicized case in Ireland where a 14-year-old rape victim was refused a termination in her country of origin. Act Of Love is standard upbeat fare lifted by its pro-choice theme, a theme already vaguely introduced by Song X, the jaunty sea-shanty-from-hell that opens Mirror Ball. It ends with an unaccompanied piece of anti-clericalism not heard since the days of Journey Through The Past in 1972, a reference to a priest with sandy hair decreeing punishments for an unspecified crime clearly sexual in origin. Young told Mark Cooper in *Q*: 'I'm personally pro-choice, but you won't hear that in the song. The song states both sides – a lot of sides – of the question. It's not up to me to write a song about what I think people should do. Then everybody can get something because all the sides are there. It's all in there.' At least Young was consistent in maintaining an anti-didactic stance.

Comparing the album track with the MTV concert with Crazy Horse, it's clear that Pearl Jam provided the leaner, tighter, more urgent backing, while the Horse fattened the song out like the wicked witch working on Hansel and Gretel. What is most impressive is the independent strength and intelligence of both Gossard and McCready, guitarists who fit like a glove around Young's playing style and, despite the legal difficulties that led Pearl Jam to be expunged from the album's sleevenotes, manage to be far more than superstar sparring partners. Act Of Love doesn't have great lyrics, although the title is ironic in an unspectacular way, rather like Throw Your Hatred Down, written in the wake of the Waco siege and a plea for peace and restraint delivered in abrasively pumped-up musical tones.

Here, the act of love could be seen as the sex act (noooo??!!), or the self-sacrifice and idealism which leads to any kind of 'holy war', be it the Crusades, fundamentalism, the anti-Federal terrorism of the Oklahoma bombing or Moral Rearmament, which leads crazily and mazily to the murder of legalized abortionists. This 'holiness' is contrasted nicely with the fragments of relationship-bullshit, especially the lines in which a man offers his wallet and warns, 'Don't call me,' to an obviously pregnant girlfriend. It sounds like the stuff wayward men get slagged off for on Jerry Springer or the Jenny Jones Show. While the word 'baby', a pop music cliché if ever there was one, is respectively linked with loss, abuse and use (exploitation), a repetition that recalls both the patronizing way in which some men, be they lovers, husbands or fathers, view some women and the child itself, which is the product of casual coupling, unwanted; as well as '*the fruit of love*' that is '*in the future*'. NY

DOWNTOWN & PEACE AND LOVE

First released: Mirror Ball (Reprise) **June 1995**

'P*eople my age/they don't do the things I do,*' warbles Neil on I'm The Ocean. No kidding. Downtown is the most ballroom-blitz-catchy number on Mirror Ball and the one that contains the title image, a revolving globe of reflected light fractured into swirling flashes, a world on a string, a song that follows From Hank To Hendrix in its conjuration of the man's contemporaries and heroes but is less of a personal odyssey than a waking dream, the past with all the bad bits taken out.

Young was inspired by his appearance at the 1995 Rock 'N' Roll Hall Of Fame ceremony, when he played with Led Zeppelin on When The Levee Breaks and was officially immortalized, in a rather silly tradition that stems from the Baseball Hall Of Fame in Cooperstown, alongside the likes of Al Green, Janis Joplin, Frank Zappa, the Allman Brothers and Led Zep themselves.

Hendrix makes another appearance in this song, '*playing in the back room*' for all the mamboing and Charlestoning hippies while Led Zeppelin are on stage, and in the most marvellously upbeat image on the entire album Young evokes '*a note from Page*' which is '*a water-washed diamond in a river of sin*', presumably not a reference to the English lads' famous antics in the clubs and bars of LA when they first got to know Young around 1970. The opening riff, which Young starts on a curse, certainly recalls the stop-everything sound of Jimmy Page who, along with singer Robert Plant, had enjoyed his own return to critically-applauded sales success with No Quarter – Unledded, a selection of old and new songs with a North African feel which made the top ten in both the US and UK album charts in late 1994. It' s an excellent record – check out Gallows Pole, straight from the annals of the Newgate Calendar, and the closing, exquisite Kashmir, recorded with a full orchestra in Marakkesh.

Oldies may recall Petula Clark's single hit of the same name from the early 1960s, but Downtown has more obvious and more poignant links with Come On Baby, Let's Go Downtown, co-authored and sung by Danny Whitten on Tonight's The Night, especially as this hymn to good times past contains salutary references to drooling doormen and the dangers of being sucked in too far. Young thought that, with the right arrangement and horn section, there might have been a hit single in here somewhere, but for him the song is a one-off, like the end of Moulin Rouge when Jose Ferrer's dying painter Henri Toulouse-Lautrec is 'visited' by all his models and friends, or a happy version of Richard III's nightmare before the last battle: 'It's like they're there,' Young told the *NME*. 'They're all there still singing and playing. It's just a place you can only go to in your mind – downtown, and whoever you like the best is going to be who's playing in the club.'

Peace and Love is almost a coda to Downtown, with Vedder's under-recorded vocals and organ from producer Brendan O'Brien acting as a muted answer to Young's memories of the 1960s: the decline of commitment, both personal and public, and the death of John Lennon, an act which is like '*a broken bell*' and one which helps to make people '*strangers in their own land*'. The song's opening refrain of '*too young to die*' links Danny Whitten with Lennon with Kurt Cobain with Pearl Jam's own Andrew Wood. While Vedder's own lyrics, hastily typed in on the sleevenotes, are nicely placed between respect and scepticism.

Sleeps With Angels reached number two in the UK and nine in the US; with Mirror Ball making it to places four and five respectively, it was arguably his most successful recording since Harvest in 1972, when Eddie Vedder was still reading Dr Seuss. NY

BIG TIME

First released: Broken Arrow (Reprise) **August 1996**
Concert version: Year Of The Horse (Shaky Films) **August 1997**

On 26 November 1995, David Briggs, co-producer on every album that Young and Crazy Horse had made together, died of lung cancer at the pitifully young age of 51. Since Young's first solo album in 1968 Briggs, along with engineer Tim Mulligan and manager's manager Elliot Roberts, had been there through times fair and foul. He would boast that he only produced 'the best' Young and from Everybody Knows This Is Nowhere through Tonight's The Night, Zuma, Ragged Glory and Weld right up to his last credit on Sleeps With Angels, he had a point.

In the *Los Angeles Times* obituary, Jimmy McDonough, one of very few writers to pierce Briggs' protective armour, quoted the man from 1991: 'Rock 'n' roll is not sedate. Is not safe. Has nothing to do with money. Rock 'n' roll is elemental – it's like wind, rain, fire. Rock 'n' roll is fire, man, "fire". It has to do with how much you can thumb you nose at the world.' It's a terrific quote, not because it says something that has never been said before but because it shows that Briggs was less of a George Martin figure than a man who could translate his passion and commitment to others, to Young, to the band.

Briggs was more like Bundini Brown to Young's Muhammed Ali, the one who told him to go out there and float and sting, and a man who believed that rock music was never better than when live and raw and immediate, of the moment, pure in intention. As a much later collaborator, guitarist with and founder of 13 Engines, John Critchley, noted in the alternative Toronto newspaper, *Now*: 'Much of his behaviour in the studio was designed to inspire those around him to reach further. Some producers will tell you that the second kick-drum beat in the seventeenth bar was late – not Briggs. He didn't care if you were out of time or out of tune, as long as the feel was right.'

Briggs was the kind of fiercely independent maverick who must have appealed to Neil from the first: even Briggs' background was the stuff of fiction. He turned his back on an abusive father, left Wyoming for the bright lights and changed his name – a fact that saw him constantly confused with the keyboardist of the same name whose Nashville House Of David was one of the recording sites for Young's Old Ways album. Tribute-makers noted Briggs' love of women, gambling and fast cars; he also had a famous penchant for feuding. Poncho Sampedro told Jim Jarmusch that Briggs 'had attitude for days'; others considered him simply too ornery to die.

Briggs was a heavy smoker and his last illness may well have been behind the reference on Mirror Ball in the song, Big Green Country, to the Marlboro Man. Certainly, it was the end of an era: as well as his obvious expertise in the recording department, Briggs was at the fore of Young's eagerly-awaited Archive project, a multi-CD retrospective which at the time of writing seems longer away than ever because of Young's oft-aired anger at the authenticity-wrecking developments in digitalized CD technology. Whatever, Briggs' role has now been taken on by Joel Bernstein, an excellent acoustic guitarist and photographer who first featured in the techno early-1980s days on vocoder.

In early 1995, Young hooked up with film-maker Jim Jarmusch, whose off-beat Western

Dead Man gave Young the chance to follow the likes of Eric Clapton and Mark Knopfler with his own film score, a 63-minute grind of wailing guitars, pump organ and tack-piano fragments. Young laid down the track while watching the film, although an early screening at the Cannes Film Festival proved slightly embarrassing. During one break in the music, an Italian journalist shouted 'Peeece of sheeet, Jim!' to cheers and applause. The film was re-edited and made fifteen minutes shorter by its release in July 1996, but though its originality pleased some, Young fared badly with the soundtrack release on his own new independent label, Vapor. Without the screen images the music floundered, like some of the more indulgent moments from Weld/Arc.

Jarmusch seemed another inevitable collaborator: a long-time fan, he was listening to Young's music and reading William Blake's poetry while making the movie; Blake even found his way into the film as the name of the central character. In images reminiscent of Pocahontas, Jarmusch told Geoff Andrew in *Time Out*: 'I got into native American culture through my grandmother, who gave me some arrowheads and stuff when I was five or six, and took me to the Great Serpent burial grounds.' When Young and Crazy Horse began work on their next album, Broken Arrow, it seemed natural that Jarmusch would direct the single video, Big Time, a song which is included here simply because it had enough clout to find its way on to that album and both the film and record versions of Year Of The Horse, different but complementary documents of Young's 1996 world tour. Big Time has a linking guitar hook which carries an intensity which belies the rather naffly sentimental lyrics and thin vocals, but at least it symbolizes the relationship that was to produce Jarmusch's documentary Year Of The Horse, one of the very finest of its kind, whether you like Young's music, Jarmusch's intelligent film-making, both or neither. And it does have another pretty sound statement of intent: *'I'm still living the dream we had/For me it's not over.'*

Jarmusch and Young have a lot in common: both are independent-minded artists, prepared to thumb their noses when it suits, and while Young is a movie-maker with a long interest in everything from actresses to directors like Jonathan Demme and Julien Temple, Jarmusch is a music nut. His best film, *Down By Law*, dragged a superb performance out of cult singer-songwriter Tom Waits (the man whose great song of futile, unrequited love, Downtown Train, was ravaged by Rod Stewart, a singer who makes Don King look introverted and lacking in confidence). The venerable Screamin' Jay Hawkins had appeared in two Jarmusch flicks and he made a much better job of a movie called *Mystery Train* in 1989 than Young did when he recorded the old Elvis Sun Sessions song on the wretched Everybody's Rockin' in 1983. Jarmusch even had the nous to cast former Clash leader Joe Strummer in the role of a gun-toting Elvis lookalike.

Frank Sampedro gave the impression that Young almost hijacked a Crazy Horse album project when Broken Arrow was put together: 'When we strapped on our instruments, after one or two takes we were done.' Sadly, and despite its evocative title, which sums up so much in Neil's life, Broken Arrow is a bridge too far for the impromptu jamming approach; a reminder that everything is subject to the law of diminishing returns. On the cassette version, the album is divided neatly between three extended jams totalling nearly twenty-six of the record's forty-eight minutes and a second side of glorified odds and sods, including the closing homage to the good old mid-1960s days of The Squires, an eight-minutes-plus live version of Jimmy Reed's 1959 blues-rocker Baby, What You Want Me To Do? with an audience sound so naturalistic that it recalls the wedding scenes in *The Deer Hunter*, almost as if Neil's saying: 'If you mothers want bootleg, I'll give you bootleg!'

It's a nice contrast to the penultimate track, Music Arcade, which is also used to close the Horse film: this is almost scratched out, a song dripping in child-like directness and honesty, a lone guitar being fingered and questions, doubts, which actually seem to mean something: '*Have you ever been lost? Have you ever been found out?*' Mirror Ball may have been a thrasher but even that had room for a 45-second interlude that ranks as the shortest-ever recorded Young song and the occasional change of pace. Broken Arrow has some good jamming on Loose Change, which turns a Bo Diddley riff into an almost hypnotic raga-like conclusion, and the aforementioned two closers: apart from that it seems almost cheap, hollow as a drum and an album that seemed to be there because the record company said it was time.

The album Year of the Horse is hardly much better: the film tracks were decided by Jarmusch; here the choice seems down to Young, his band and Elliot Roberts, and given the staggering amount of unreleased live material available elsewhere it's hard to credit how so-so these selections are. Nothing to approach Down By The River or All Along The Watchtower or the startlingly fresh version of Blowing In The Wind from Weld. Only the closer, Sedan Delivery, on which Young tells the crowd to 'smell the Horse on this one', has any real punch to it, although Jarmusch says that he wanted to include Prisoners (Of Rock 'N' Roll) in the movie.

This song may be sub-rebel-yell dreck from Life but its defiant opener is at least in keeping with the spirit of the film. Of the ultimate Young and Horse album, Ragged Glory, only Fuckin' Up is included, and that only in the film, albeit in a version powered by candid personal revelation, Young dressed Pearl Jam-style in ballooning shorts like some ageing geek, screaming into the mike: *'It brings back the day when my daddy walked up to me and said, "You're never going to be no good. You're just a fuck up, a fuck up, a fuck up".'* Maybe that kind of stuff was considered too 'of-the-moment' for an album.

Of the eleven songs on the Horse album, only four appear in the film and all in different versions. Indeed, despite occasional footage from the tour, shots of the crowd, of the skyline and rolling hills, the concert material, the film's real highlight, is taken from only two concerts: the Gorge in Washington State, and the Antique Theatre in Vienne, France, outside Lyon, a first century AD amphitheatre. Year Of The Horse was the third live album that Young had made with Crazy Horse but the film, with its mix of home movie retrospective and excitingly visceral live footage shot on grainy super 8, is of a different order to anything Young had done in the past. Young told *Time Out New York*: 'I love 16mm or 8mm through a long lens, through atmosphere – smoke and stuff. It's kind of more like painting than a snapshot. There's something left open for you. Your imagination can make more of a natural, chemical interpretation of the light.'

Jarmusch's film avoids voiceover or any kind of narrative, while the music clips almost wholly try to reproduce the concert-going experience, close-up largely giving way to middle-distance tableaux in which the band's collective in-a-ring work takes on its own momentum. The film uses interviews, most of them conducted in a nondescript room with a washing machine in the corner, and though the rock clichés abound it's much to the director's credit that he propels Crazy Horse to the front, so much so that Young is quite credible when he states that he sees himself as the guitar player with the band rather than (presumably) its star. Sampedro shines in particular, both in his own personal revelations about his own drug habit and his confrontations with Jarmusch who he dismisses at one point as 'an artsy fartsy film-maker' and a 'producer' from New York. Though Jarmusch corrects him on the last point, he has considerable balls to include Sampedro's mocking belief that such a film will only scratch the surface of a band that's been together through close on thirty years.

Jarmusch is too smart to ignore the Spinal Tap connections and to his credit Young has always noted them himself (when he summoned the Horse at the time of Ragged Glory, he told *Rolling Stone* that 'Nigel is back in the band'). Old footage from the Young personal collection includes the band rather pathetically setting fire to some artificial flowers in a Glasgow hotel in 1976; smoking and extolling the joys of dope and almost coming to blows after a Rotterdam gig in 1986; Young's sense of humour also comes across when he is collared again in 1976 London by a self-styled Jesus-impersonator: 'Well, we gotta go. Nice talking to you, Jesus. I hope you make it this time. Last time it was kinda rough.' Critics were less kind about a conversation between Young and Jarmusch on the 1996 tour bus when Young asked the film-maker to explain the difference between the Old and New Testament. 'The Old Testament is where God is really pissed, right?' You have to be a rock legend to ask stuff like that, right?!

But even the ever-sceptical Jonathan Romney, who mocked this in the *Guardian* when the film was premiered in London as part of the London Film Festival, enthused: 'The concert footage is nothing short of incendiary. For over twenty years, Young and his grizzled crew have refuted the truism that rock 'n' roll is a sadly undignified business once you hit thirty – here, proto-punk thrashers like Fuckin' Up and Sedan Delivery remind you where Sonic Youth and a thousand Seattle brats got their schooling.'

As The Grateful Dead have said, what a long strange trip it's all been, this career of Young's that Jarmusch wonderfully concertinas in one sublime take which cuts from the Hammersmith Odeon in 1976 to a gig twenty years on, Like A Hurricane with almost the same voice and the same old 1952 Les Paul guitar, admittedly with a lot of fretwork and assorted improvements in between. Even of late, Neil's life continues to be eventful. His love of trains both ancient and modern and his commitment to his family took on a whole new dimension in 1995 when he became a part-owner of the model outfit, Lionel Trains. He has since developed a remote control device that allows the severely handicapped, like his sons Ben, now 19, and Zeke, 25, to participate in the joys of braking or sounding horns simply by moving their head. Indeed, his long, distinguished career (with wife Pegi and manager Roberts) of work with the Bridge School has culminated in the Reprise release, The Bridge School Concerts, a fraction of the music performed at these events since the mid-1980s but about as inspired as any 'charity record' could be. Young's moving opener I Am A Child is matched by an amazing version of Heroes by David Bowie, Simon And Garfunkel reprising America, Elvis Costello reminding us of the links between Alison and Down By The River and Patti Smith closing these fifteen tracks with The People Have The Power. (Anyone interested in learning more about or contributing to the Bridge School can write to 545 Eucalyptus Avenue, Hillsborough, Ca 94010). The sleeve is filled with photos of the children, kids who have obviously been touched by Young and his family just as much as they have helped him to become the man that he so obviously is today: not perfect, but the kind of guy who's special in a way that we can appreciate and cope with: sane, happy, productive, a soul survivor – just hear those friendly, unobtrusive, undemanding shouts from the crowd at so many concerts. 'Neil! Hey, Neil!' It's what you'd shout across a bar to a long-lost friend. Or that guy you once had a crush on.

On 12 October 1996, Young played at the tenth Farm Aid benefit in Columbia, South Carolina, and talked mordantly about how, after a decade, 'we have now got it down to 500 farms a week', referring to the current run of closures. His stand against corporate rock continued in May 1997, when he refused to be inducted into the Rock 'N' Roll Hall Of Fame as part of Buffalo Springfield because of the price of $1,500 charged to family members of inductees and the Hall's selling of rights to broadcast highlights to the cable station, VH1. Young was supported by David Crosby, himself a past inductee as a member of The Byrds!

In June 1997, he was in the news again when a five-week European tour was cancelled after Young had cut his chord-making index finger on his left hand. Amusingly, the incident was variously reported as the result of a failed ham-sandwich incision or a botched attempt to open one of those impenetrable turkey-loaf plastic packs (Piece Of Crap?). Ironically, Bob Dylan went down with a serious heart complaint at the same time, and as well as upstaging Young's accident Dylan's no-show at various European festivals would have meant a call-up for Young if it hadn't been for the cut. No wonder Young joked to the *Chicago Tribune*: 'It's macaroni cheese from now on.' Dylan was eventually replaced at London's Finsbury Park's annual Fleadh bash by Shane MacGowan, who sang Danny Boy with all the style that sees drunks thrown out of pubs all over the world! Dylan was to pay tribute to Neil on his best album in years, Time Out Of Mind (1997). On the last track, Highlands, he confesses to listening to Young with everyone telling him to turn down the volume.

Of course, Young soon bounced back: in the summer of 1997, he toured across America with HORDE (Horizons Of Rock Developing Everywhere), a festival on legs founded six years previously by members of Blues Traveler for essentially roots and retro bands of all persuasions. Neil obviously revelled in it, playing solo sets in the morning as well as scene-stealing evening gigs with Crazy Horse, being reminded of the old Buffalo Springfield days crisscrossing the broad, brown land with The Doors or The Turtles, and no doubt chuffed to be the granddaddy to offspring as various as Beck, Primus, Leftover Salmon, New Brown Hat and England's own Kula Shaker. From Salt Lake City to Scranton, Pa., from Miami to Milwaukee. Rockin' In The Free World. Forever Young. NY

GEORGE NICHOPOLOUS
Elvis A. Presley
Graceland, Memphis

Essential

Neil Young

Appendix

ESSENTIAL NEIL YOUNG DISCOGRAPHY

Buffalo Springfield (Atlantic, January, 1967)
Buffalo Springfield Again (Atlantic, December, 1967)
Neil Young (January, 1968 Reprise, as are all unless stated)
Everybody Knows This Is Nowhere (May, 1969)
After The Goldrush (August, 1970)
Harvest (Feb, 1972)
On The Beach (July, 1974)
Tonight's The Night (June, 1975)
American Stars And Bars (June, 1977)
Comes A Time (September, 1978)
Rust Never Sleeps (June, 1979)
Trans (Geffen, January, 1983)
Old Ways (Geffen, August, 1985)
This Note's For You (April, 1988)
Freedom (October, 1989)
Ragged Glory (September, 1990)
Harvest Moon (Nov, 1992)
Sleeps With Angels (September, 1994)
Mirror Ball (June, 1995)

TEN YOUNG COVERS

The Wayward Wind
All Along The Watchtower
Blowin' In The Wind
Mystery Train
On Broadway
Farmer John
Dock Of The Bay
Rainin' In My Heart
Betty Lou's Got A Brand New Pair Of Shoes
Baby, What You Want Me To Do

TEN ESSENTIAL COVERS OF YOUNG SONGS

Flaming Lips After the Goldrush (The Bridge, 1988)
The Mint Juleps Only Love Can Break Your Heart (7" single)
Loop Cinammon Girl (The Bridge)
Nick Cave Helpless (The Bridge)
Annie Lennox Don't Let It Bring You Down (Medusa, 1995)
Nicolette Larson Lotta Love (7", 1979)
Sonic Youth Computer Age (The Bridge)
The Alarm Rockin' In The Free World (Raw, 1991)
Cowboy Junkies Powderfinger (The Caution Horses, 1990)
The Dave Clark Five Southern Man (7" single)

THE ESSENTIAL NEIL YOUNG BIBLIOGRAPHY

For What It's Worth: The Story Of Buffalo Springfield by John Einarson and Richie Furay **Quarry Press, Kingston, Ontario, 1997**

Don't Be Denied: Neil Young – The Canadian Years by John Einarson **Omnibus, London, 1993**

Neil Young: The Man And His Music by David Downing **Bloomsbury, London, 1994**

Neil And Me by Scott Young **Rogan House, London, 1997**

Ghosts On The Road: Neil Young In Concert by Pete Long **The Old Homestead Press, London, 1996**

Neil Young And Broken Arrow: On A Journey Through The Past edited by Alan Jenkins **Neil Young Appreciation Society, Bridgend, Wales, 1994**

Crosby, Stills, Nash And Young: The Visual Documentary by Johnny Rogan **Omnibus, London, 1996**

The Complete Guide To The Music Of Neil Young by Johnny Rogan **Omnibus, London, 1996**

Love To Burn: Thirty Years Of Speaking Out by Paul Williams **Omnibus, London, 1997**

Neil Young: The Rolling Stone Files edited by Holly George-Warren **Pan, London, 1994**

Neil Young: The Visual Documentary by John Robertson **Omnibus, London, 1994**

AND ALSO

As well as the above, the following books were invaluable in provoking thought on various aspects of Neil Young's life and work:

Waiting For The Sun by Barney Hoskyns **Viking, London, 1996**

Crosstown Traffic: Jimi Hendrix and Post-War Pop by Charles Shaar Murray **Faber, London, 1989**

Helter Skelter by Victor Buglioso **Norton, New York, 1974**

Flashman And The Redskins by George MacDonald Fraser **Collins, London, 1982**

Chasin' The Trane by JC Thomas **Doubleday New York, 1974**

The Great Rock Discography compiled by MC Strong **Canongate, Edinburgh, 1996**

ALSO AVAILABLE IN THIS SERIES

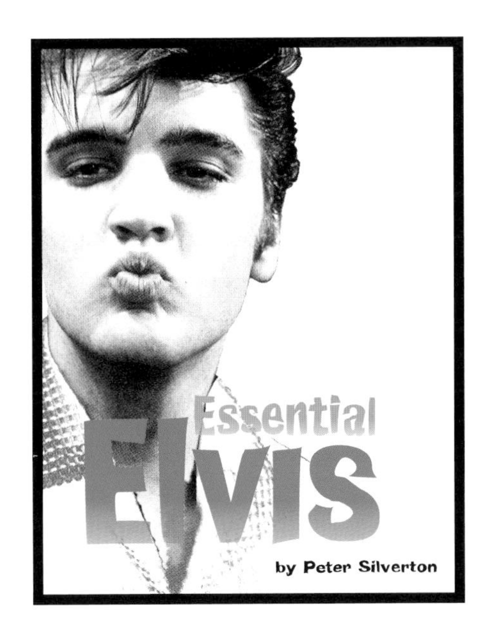

Essential Elvis
Peter Silverton
ISBN: 0 233 99245 6
Price: £12.99

Essential Elton
Spencer Bright
ISBN: 0 233 99361 4
Price: £12.99

PICTURE CREDITS

Chuck Boyd/FC/Redferns ************************** P7, 45
Michael Putland/Retna ****************************** P11
G. Hanekroot/Sunshine/Retna ********************** P14, 22
Michael Ochs Archives/Redferns ********************* P17, 42
Mathew Taylor/Animals Unlimited ******* P25, 30, 33, 51, 54, 57, 61, 65
Redferns *********************************** P26
Dick Barnatt/Redferns ***************************** P35
Richie Aaron/Redferns ****************************** P38
Neal Preston/Retna ***************************** P46, 66
Corbis-Bettmann-UPI ******************************* P49
Ebert Roberts/Redferns **************** P63, 86, 89, 91, 93, 105
Animals Unlimited ******************** P68, 71, 75, 78, 83, 98
Roy Tee ©89/SIN ********************************* P94
Peter Tangen/Retna ****************************** P97
AJ Barratt/Retna ********************************* P109
Mick Hutson/Redferns ***************************** P110
Jay Blakesberg/Retna ****************************** P113
Richard Beland/SIN ******************************** P120